ELECTRIC SMOKER COOKBOOK

Exploit Your Electric Smoker With Over 200 Easy-To-Follow, Irresistible Recipes For Beginners + Tips On Cooking Times, Temperatures, Quality & Quantity Of Wood Chips

Author Name:
Mike Cook

©Copyright 2021 Mike Cook - All Rights Reserved.

Table Of Contents

Mike Cook

Introduction

Electric smokers are a safe way to make sure you have the meat that you want, as well as the smoky flavor you desire. Smokers are sold in a lot of stores like Wal-Mart and Goodwill. They are also sold online. They can also be purchased from certain internet sources. All of these smokers are very easy to use. They require very little time and patience to learn and operate. This will also allow you to have fun cooking and learning new things.

Electric smokers very quickly provide the option to smoke meats through an easy-to-use and accessible interface. This design allows a lot of people to participate in the fun of smoking meats. This is a trend more people are jumping on, and they are becoming more and more popular.

These smokers are considered to be modern-day smokers. The way it works is it uses electricity to heat the inside of the smoker. That heat is what cooks the meats and creates a smoky flavor.

In truth, you can smoke meats in just about anything. The pros will say that, for meat smoking, the primarily important thing is temperature control. Rather than smoking meats in a smoker, have a look at some of these options instead. Some of the most popular methods for smoking meats involve ice, water, and wood or charcoal to reduce the meat's temperature below the smoke generator's smoke generator while allowing for ventilation of the heat from the smoke generator.

Also, it uses moist heat instead of dry heat. The result is wet smoke that is considered to be more flavorful than dry smoke. This type of smoker looks like a makeshift wooden box with all kinds of holes and gaps. It has a lid made from clear plastic so people can monitor the meat throughout the cooking process. They can be hung from a ceiling or mounted on a table.

The smoke outlet is a hole in the top of the smoker. There will also be a tray that collects the drops of fat and grease. This tray will need to be emptied after the cooking process is complete. If you are thinking of getting an electric smoker, you should have read this book. There are some very useful facts here.

They are also easy to use, which is probably the biggest reason they are becoming more popular. Unlike other smokers, electric smokers don't have to be monitored at all times. They don't need to be held up to burn a fire on the bottom. Everything is done for them once they are plugged in.

The smoking process and the results people get are very enjoyable. Many different types of meats and vegetables can be cooked with this type of smoker. They are very popular with most people because they are relatively inexpensive and easy to use.

One thing to remember about these smokers is that they are a lot different from many smokers that you have experienced in the past. For example, you will not have the artificial heat from the fire that comes from a barrel smoker. It does not have to be as hot as a regular smoker. All you have to worry about is having it plugged in and just waiting for the time to pass.

CHAPTER 1:

Going Electric

Time

Unlike grilling or even barbequing, smoking takes a really long time and requires a whole lot of patience. It takes time for the smoky flavor to get infused into the meats slowly. To bring things into comparison, it takes about 8 minutes to thoroughly cook a steak through direct heating, while smoking (indirect heating) will take around 35 to 40 minutes.

Temperature

When it comes to smoking, the temperature is affected by many different factors limited to the wind, cold air temperatures, and the cooking wood's dryness. Some smokers work best with large fires controlled by the draw of a chimney and restricted airflow through the various vents of the cooking chamber and firebox.

At the same time, other smokers tend to require smaller fire with fewer coals and a completely different combination of the vent and draw controls. However, most smokers are designed to work at temperatures as low as 180 °F to as high as 300 °F. But the recommended temperature usually falls between 250 °F and 275 °F.

Your electric smoker gives you the choice of cooking a complete meal all at once or smoking a large quantity of a single meat, fish, or vegetable for batch cooking. The slightly humid environment of an electric smoker means no more dried-out meats, and the low temperature allows connective tissue and fats to melt away, giving you that juicy barbecue you love so much. And the smoker's drip tray will catch the drippings, so cleanup isn't a nightmare. The next time you crave a tender pulled pork or thinly sliced brisket, make it yourself!

However, more than allowing you to make delicious smoked foods in a breeze, there are so many benefits of using this type of electric smoker, for example:

Ease of operation: You don't need to be a kitchen expert in order to use the Electric Smoker. It is very simple to operate. Once you have loaded the meat or food inside the smoker, all it takes is to set the temperature and time and wait until it is cooked.

The electric energy source is neutral: Even if this particular electric smoker uses electricity as its energy source, it does not leave a flavor of its own. This means that whatever wood you use will be the only flavoring in the food. The energy source will never contaminate the taste that you desire.

Easy cleanup: This type of electric smoker is effortless to clean. You are not required to use cleaners for the interior of the electric smoker. What makes it trouble-free to clean is that there are no messy charcoal ashes to empty or a propane tank to remove.

No need to babysit the cooking: Since you can digitally control both time and temperature, you don't need to watch your cooking. This means that you can do other things while your food cooks.

The smoking unit has a large capacity: The smoking unit has a hefty capacity, so you can fill it with wood to cook a large volume of foods. This lets you avoid opening the electric smoker to refill with more wood.

The most notable characteristic of an electric smoker is its shape. Electric smokers all share a unique tall and narrow shape, referred to as a box, cabinet, locker, or block smoker, because of the heat source. Located in the base, the electric heating element radiates heat, which naturally rises to the top of the smoker. Then, as the heat cools slightly it creates convection. Convection moves heat in waves throughout the insulated box. The insulation in an electric smoker is an important quality, as it directly affects the smoker's ability to contain heat. Although high heat is not associated with smoking, consistent heat is paramount. The electrical efficiency, wood consumption, cooking time, and even smoking temperature are all variables controlled by the insulation

The smoker's electric heating element starts with the press of a button located on the digital control panel, which also includes a cooking timer and precise temperature and smoke regulators. Access to the perforated or wire sliding trays is easy, and the adjustable shelving allows for a variety of food sizes—whether multiple trays of chicken wings or a single large turkey.

Smoking Pantry And Smoking Terms

The art of smoking comes complete with its own lexicon of terms, as with any vocation or avocation, and the first thought you need to know is the distinction between barbecue, grilling, and smoking. First of all, while "grill" and "barbecue" are sometimes used interchangeably, they are not exactly the same thing. And while you can use a grill as a smoker, and smoke is flavored with barbecued beef, smoking and grilling are also not the same thing.

But as complicated as it sounds, it's not. The basic thumb rule is: while smoking is slow and low, grilling is fast and hot.

Barbecuing is normally done on a grill, but you cook it at a lower temperature (around 300-500 degrees Fahrenheit) when you "barbecue" food than when you grill food. Grilling is a fast-cooking process with high heat (above 500 degrees) that seals the outside of the meat and seals the juices inside.

Burning, on the other hand, is typically a method of exposing ingredients to smoke at a low heat (under 140 degrees). It is a system that can take hours, or as long as several weeks, to complete. Hot Smoking," which is a method that simultaneously roasts and flavors the meat at temperatures above 140 degrees, is the exception." Food that is' hot smoked' is fully cooked.

'Cold smoked' food, normally cheese (which will ooze and melt at higher temperatures) or fish, usually between 68-90 degrees Fahrenheit, is cooked at a much lower temperature.

Here are a few other terms for smoking you might encounter in conversations:

AMNPS: is the Amaze-N-Pellet Smoker's proprietary shorthand, a portable smoke generator that burns either sawdust or pellets (made from compressed sawdust) and works for both hot and cold smoking.

Bark: the crunchy, fatty crust that develops when it is heated past 300 degrees on the outside of the meat, setting off the "Maillard Reaction."

Brine: is a salting process that is either a "wet brine" or "dry" (salt rubbed into the food) (salt mixed with water and sometimes spices). In the smoking process, brining meat (particularly poultry) will help keep it moist.

Chimney: a cylindrical device used without lighter fluid to help ignite charcoal, which can add toxic chemicals to smoke and the meat has a terrible taste.

Cheap Offset Smoker

Dalmatian Rub—salt and pepper

EOS-refers to a costly offset smoker

A derogatory term for propane-fueled smokers, typically spoken by those who claim that the use of electric and gas-fueled smokers is "cheating".

L.P: the liquid propane gas used to power grills and smokers. Usually available at 20-lb in bottles.

Maillard Reaction-a chemical process that occurs when foods are browned between 285-330 degrees Fahrenheit. The crunchy layer (known among barbecue enthusiasts as "bark") that forms on the outside of a seared piece of meat as the golden-brown crust on baked bread is responsible for this process.

Montreal-style: smoked meat is produced by salting and curing beef brisket with salt and spices and then hot-smoked and steamed. It is similar to pastrami and it is prepared in almost the same way.

Reverse Sear: using indirect heat in the middle of a piece of meat to increase the temperature.

The stage at which fat starts to smoke, Smoke Point, will differ by content. Although ghee (clarified butter) has a smoke point of 485 degrees, butter has a low smoke point (about 325 degrees).

A smoker designed to use burning logs as fuel is a stick burner.

Smoking Gear and Equipment

- Gas Grills

The industry has a lot of gas-fired smokers and there are pros and cons of using them. One downside is that if you smoke long, slowly, propane is not a cost-efficient fuel. That's where smokers like the MasterBuilt Pro (under $200) with "dual fuel."

Pros: Gas smokers can be used and managed very quickly. Smokers with gas-fired cabinets are especially easy to clean.

Cons: propane fuel generates "clean heat" but a chemical is added to it for protection since it is odorless. The issue is that there is a distinctive and unpleasant scent of this compound. It is not so much a concern to use propane in outdoor barbecue grills since the smell dissipates in the open air, however the smell will end up in the meat being smoked when used in a smoker's sealed setting.

- Charcoal kettle

These are the familiar barbecues that have been populating backyards for decades, black-enameled. By closing the lid and using indirect heat to smoke your products, they can be turned into "smokers," but you can also purchase purpose-built barbecue accessories such as the "Smokenator," which is installed into a charcoal kettle and converts it into a water smoker, keeping temperatures low and even and keeping food moist as it smokes.

Pros: In contrast to purpose-built smokers and high-end barbecues, traditional charcoal kettles are lightweight, compact, and affordable.

Cons: To sustain the heat, charcoal needs to be added every hour or so and it can be tricky to keep the temperature steady.

- Electric Smokers

Both sizes and shapes come with electric smokers. Others have enough computer-controlled technology, such as the Cookshack Amerique ($2300), that you can smoke a brisket and launch the space shuttle at the same time, while others have less than $500, such as the Bradley Smokers Original Smoker, which smokes cold and hot, roasts and dries food.

Pros: With their temperature ranges, electric smokers are not only versatile: hot smoking, cold smoking, plain-old barbecue, but they also have a degree of automation that makes the process simpler and "cleaner" than most smokers. Some are simply "set it and forget it" while a lot of attention is required for smokers shot by more conventional fuel.

Cons: Price. Electric smokers are costly to purchase and expensive to restore.

- Vertical Box smoker

These are straightforward in construction and stable. Prices may differ and the boxes may not be as well sealed at the lower end of the price scale, resulting in temperature variations. Most experts would tell you to go for the water smoker if you have an option between a vertical box smoker and a vertical water smoker at approximately the same price.

Pros: Portability, especially compared to sometimes unwieldy offset smokers.

Cons: They're not as flexible as other smokers and make bad grills, in particular. The meat can also be more difficult to reach when it's cooking

- Water smoker

Three specific elements are designed for these smokers: a chamber for the source of fuel, a water pan, and then room for the food you smoke.

The cheapest smokers you can purchase are the Vertical Water Smokers. (One of the most famous brands sells for less than $100) and these are the market's best-selling smokers, overall. They are pretty easy to use as well. Charcoal, electricity or a gas burner will power them, and all that is required is to fill the water pan and then ignite or turn the fuel source on. Add the meat and that's it.

Pros: These smokers are tiny and take up very little real estate. They are more fuel effective than larger smokers as well.

Cons: You will not manage the smoke as well as you can with other forms of smokers while using a small water smoker, so there is a greater chance of creosote building up on your smoked food.

• Offset Barrel smoker

For novices, these smokers can be tricky, so you should actually have some time under your belt before buying one. Timber or charcoal is used to fuel them.

"Offset barrel smokers", also referred to as "pipe smokers", "horizontal smokers", or "stick-burners" used to dominate smoking/barbecue events in the competition.

The "offset" smoker is placed lower (or often in the back) of the cooking chamber where the food is smoked. This implies that the heat is not directly beneath, but next to, the food.

Brinkmann makes many models of their Offset smokers and they all come in at under $300, making this style of smoker one of the most affordable. Some consumers have complained, on the downside, that the lower-priced smokers are too small for big work, such as smoking a turkey.

High-end offset smokers are made of thicker metal ($800 and up) and can have low, even, radiant heat.

Pros: Offset smokers allow you to smoke meat cuts that are larger than a vertical smoker. It is also possible to use offset smokers as grills, though vertical smokers are not really intended for that assignment.

Cons: More cost-effective offset smoker brands appear to have leaky fireboxes that can make it hard to control airflow. A tendency for the paint to flake and the metal to rust are other documented issues.

• Kama do-Style smoker

Inspired by traditional wood/charcoal-burning cookers (originally clay pots) used for centuries in Japan, these modern-day smokers are made of a variety of materials, including ceramics, steel, terracotta, and a mixture of cement and crushed rock. One of the best-known smokers of this kind is the omnipresent BGE (Big Green Egg).

Pros: The advanced venting system helps airflow to be precise. Fans of this smoker's style admire its versatility. The construction allows for extreme heat (up to 750 degrees) so that you can also bake, in addition to grilling and smoking.

Cons: Price. With price tags beginning at just under a thousand and going up to what you would expect to pay for a used car, these smokers are pricey.

Safety

If you've ever cooked fried chicken in a skillet of cast iron, you know that so much smoke will kick in the process that you'll be tempted to disconnect your smoke alarm.

You may worry that it is messy or downright unhealthy to smoke indoors. Only make sure you follow the instructions on whatever gadget you're using to smoke indoors and make sure the kitchen fan is on!

Oven-roasting-style smokers and Stove-Top kettle smokers have many choices for smoking indoors.

General Food Safety

In making sure your food is safe, common sense is your best ally. Always ensure that your area of food preparation is safe. Before handling raw meat, wash your hands, especially chicken, which is notorious for being an incubator of bad bacteria.

In between applications, sterilize cutting boards and wash knives.

Make sure it's covered in airtight containers while storing smoked food in the freezer.

Process Of Using Electric Smoker

Now, the good news for all of your smoke aficionados out there is that using an Electric Smoker isn't exactly rocket science! This means anyone will be able to use it, following some very basic and simple guidelines. So it is crucial that you go through this section before starting to smoke your meat. After all, you don't want your expensive cut to be ruined just because of some silly mishap right?

Just follow the basics and you will be fine!

- The first step is to make sure that you always wear safety gloves
- Take out the chips tray and add your wood chips (before smoking begins)
- However, once the smoking has started, you can easily use the side chip tray for adding your chips
- The additional chips are required to infuse the meat with a more smoky flavor
- Once the chip bay is ready, load up your marinated meat onto the grill directly
- The stainless steel rack is made for direct smoking; however, if you wish they you can use a stainless steel container to avoid drippings
- Once the meat is in place, lock the door of the chamber
- Turn your smoker "On" using the specified button and adjust the temperature
- Wait until it is done!

Keep in mind that the above-mentioned steps are merely the basic ones; different recipes might call for different steps to follow.

Either way, they won't be much complicated as well!

CHAPTER 2:

Feed your Smoke

Troubleshooting And Smoker Maintenance

Electric smokers are incredibly convenient. You'll want to be prepared to deal with accidents and other issues which can be minimize following the set out manual available for Electric smoker. Each electric smoker owner's manual has official information on safety, troubleshooting, and maintenance. Let's take a look at the few needed to troubleshoot:

The Electric Smoker Is Not Starting Up

1. Unplug the cord from its electrical socket. Then press the power on the button, usually located in the front, under the hood, to check if it will start.
2. Check if there is a faulty plug connection on the electric cord and wall socket, and replace it or repair it.
3. Check if there's a weak battery in the smoker. If so, replace the battery.
4. Check if there are dirty or broken starting switches and clean or replace them.
5. Check if there is a loose wire from the starter and repair or replace it.
6. Check if the temperature/pressure controller is broken and replace or repair it.
7. Check if the primary air tubes are blocked or broken, clean them, or repair them.
8. Check if there is a cut-off valve and check if it is working or replace it.

Cold Smoking Safety Basics

In order to ensure that foodborne parasites such as ringworm and tapeworm are destroyed, food must show a core temperature of 140 degrees for a full minute while it is cold smoked. It might also not be enough to kill off all parasites if the cold smoking process has been combined with salting. To destroy these parasites, the FDA recommends freezing food (particularly salmon) at a temperature of minus 4 degrees Fahrenheit.

Wood To Be Used And Avoided

If you decide to use wood, you have some choices to make and some questions to ask:

In a smoker/barbecue, would you use wood of some kind? Oh, no. Softwoods like pine not only burn too rapidly, but when the aromatic resins in the wood evaporate into the smoke, they can also ruin the taste of your food. Not only will that, but the sticky residue left behind by the atomized resins ruin your smoker's interior. Stick to hardwoods such as oak, maple, hickory, and mesquite.

Which one will be better, chips or chunks? Many professional pit-masters would claim chunks are best. In the same amount of time that three or four medium-sized pieces of hardwood burn, you can use up a whole bag of chips.

Is soaking wood/chips really important before using them?

Conventional wisdom maintains that you simply have to soak chips and bits of wood, and several old smoke ology books. In the old days, soaking wood stopped it from catching on fire and damaging the food with creosote and other deposits until grills and smokers made for more reliable temperatures. The danger is almost non-existent now, particularly with gas and electric smokers, and even in wood-fueled smokers, chips and chunks in well-insulated fire pans or in a foil pouch should not catch fire.

Wood chips combination and food Recipes

Wood chips							
Alder	Poultry	Fish	Beef	Pork	Vegetables	Lamb	Turkey
Almond	Poultry						Turkey
Apple	Poultry		Beef	Pork	Vegetables	Lamb	
Cherry	Poultry	Fish	Beef	Pork		Lamb	Turkey
Mulberry							
Hazelnut	Poultry			Pork			
Hickory	Poultry		Beef	Pork			Turkey
Pecan	Poultry		Beef	Pork	Vegetables		Turkey
Maple	Poultry	Fish	Beef	Pork			Turkey
Walnut					Vegetables		
Orange and Lemon	Poultry		Beef	Pork			
Herbs	Poultry				Vegetables		
Coconut							
Oak		Fish	Beef				
Apricot					Vegetables		
Lilac		Fish				Lamb	
Grape vines	Poultry					Lamb	
Birch	Poultry			Pork			
Guava	Poultry	Fish	Beef	Pork			

How often to add wood chips

Considering all of the considerations above, let's eventually talk about how much your electric smoker will add wood chips. First, check your manual to approximately understand how long your unique model can smoke with a complete wood chip tray, as this gives you a rough idea of how frequently to add them.

Fire up your smoker and do a dry run to find out what it was like. Season your electric smoker without adding any food if it is fresh, and after 2 hours, add the chips to the tray and time for how long it produces smoke. This then provides you with the time to know when to fill it up again. If it produces 2 hours of smoke, but for 4 hours, you want to smoke your food, then you simply fill it halfway through again. You need to add more wood chips every hour for six hours if you want to smoke something for 6 hours, but it's only worth 1 hour. It's truly as easy as that!

Mind, as we say, you can not smoke for more than six hours, even though your smoker is willing to smoke for 8 hours. After 6 hours, simply remove the tray, and any unburned chips can be saved for the smoking next.

<h1 style="text-align:center">CHAPTER 3:</h1>

Smoking Time and Temperatures

The time and temperature for smoking temperatures are dependent on the type of meat to be cooked and, most notably, the cut of meat being used. Smokers are usually heated up to 250°F. Smoke is produced when wood chips burn. The smoking time of Electric smoker is not a rapid process. For example, three hours of smoking time will produce two pounds of meat in the best case. Hence, high heat smoking is not recommended on a fresh burger patty. Waits of up to 3 hours for cooking larger portions are not unusual. Smoking times are also dependent on the Electric smoker's temperature. The higher the Electric smoker temperature, the shorter the smoking time. For example, an Electric smoker temperature of 250°F will produce smoke in a shorter time than if the temperature is at 350°F. Here's a table for a better understanding of smoking time and temperature. All smoking time are implied in per pound.

Items to Smoke	Temperature	Time for Smoking	Internal Temperature
Salmon	250 °F	2 Hours	145 °F
Chicken	350 °F	30 Minutes	170 °F
Tuna	250 °F	1 Hour	125 °F
Oyster	225 °F	15 Minutes	To Taste
Bell Pepper	225 °F	1 Hour 30 Minutes	Until Tender
Corn	450 °F	15 Minutes	Until It's Tender and Soft
Onion	250 °F	2 Hours	Until Soft and Tender
Crab	200 °F	15 Minutes	170 °F
Peach	225 °F	35 Minutes	To Taste
Potato	400 °F	50 Minutes	Until Crispy
Pineapple	250 °F	1 Hour	To Taste
Squash	225 °F	1 Hour	Until Tender

| Sausage | 225 °F | 1 Hour 30 Minutes | 160 °F |

Lamb Chop	165 To 450 °F from Smoke to Sear	10 to 20 Minutes	145 °F
Lamb Rack	275 °F	1 Hour 30 Minutes	145 °F
Turkey	250 °F	30 Minutes	165 °F
Turkey Legs	225 °F	4 to 5 Hours	165 °F
Baby Back Ribs	225 °F	5 Hours	190 °F
Pork Shoulder	225 °F	10 Hours	205 °F
Pork Chops	325 °F	45 Minutes	160 °F
Pork Loin	250 °F	3 Hours	160 °F
Tenderloin	400 °F	30 Minutes	120 °F
Texas Shoulder	250 °F	12 Minutes	195 °F
Artichokes	225 °F	2 Hours	165 °F

CHAPTER 4:

Poultry Recipes

1. Smoked Chicken Legs

Preparation Time: 30 minutes
Cooking Time: 2 hours
Servings: 3
Ingredients:

- 6 chicken legs
- 1 cup olive oil
- 1 tbsp. cayenne pepper
- 1 tbsp. paprika
- 2 tbsp. salt
- 1 tbsp. onion powder
- 1 tbsp. dried thyme
- 1 tbsp. garlic powder
- 1 tbsp. pepper

Directions:

1. Start your smoker up half an hour before you start cooking.
2. Stir together all the dry ingredients. Be sure to rub the olive oil all over the chicken legs.
3. Now rub the seasoning over the chicken legs until they're fully coated.
4. Place the chicken legs on the smoking rack.
5. Turn them over so they cook evenly. You may have to add more smoker chips as you do this. Smoke Temp: 220

Nutrition:
Calories 1053
Total Fat 100g
Saturated Fat 9.8g
Cholesterol 0mg
Sodium 1555mg
Total Carbohydrate 12.1g
Dietary Fiber 2.6g
Total Sugars 2g
Protein 35.6g
Vitamin D 0mcg
Calcium 45mg
Iron 3mg
Potassium 177mg

2. Smoked Chicken Wings With Herbs

Preparation Time: 10 minutes
Cooking Time: 1 hour
Servings: 5
Ingredients:

- 5 Pounds of chicken wings
- ½ Cup of extra virgin olive oil
- 1/3 Cup of chopped fresh basil leaves
- 2 Tablespoons of chopped fresh rosemary leaves
- 2 Tablespoons of thyme leaves or fresh oregano
- 2 Large minced garlic cloves
- The juice of 1 small lime or lemon
- 1 and ½ teaspoons of sea salt
- 1 Teaspoon of freshly ground black pepper

Directions:

1. Start by rinsing the chicken wings under cool water and pat dry with clean paper towels
2. Cut the tips of the wings and cut the wings into half at the joints

3. Place the portions of the wings in a large bowl or a baking dish.

4. Mix the herbs with the garlic, the lemon, the salt and the pepper

5. Add half the marinade to the wings and mix it very well with both your hands; then set the chicken wings and mix with both your hands; then set the other half of the marinade aside for the serving

6. Close the dish with a plastic wrap then place it in the refrigerator for about 1 to 4 hours.

7. Move the chicken away from the refrigerator about 30 minutes before smoking it.

8. Take a rack or 2 racks of your smoker and place it on top of the counter; then add the mild wood chips; like alder chips to the tray of your electric smoker

9. Fill the water bowl half way; then open the top of the vent and Heat the smoker to a temperature of about 250° F

10. Place the racks of the wings in your electric smoker and smoke for about 1 hour.

11. Check the temperature with a meat thermometer for an internal temperature that is about 165° F

12. Serve and enjoy your delicious dish!

Nutrition:
Calories 1051 Total Fat 54.2g
Saturated Fat 12.3g Cholesterol 404mg
Sodium 953mg Total Carbohydrate 3.8g
Dietary Fiber 1.8g Total Sugars 0.4g
Protein 131.8g
Calcium 123mg Iron 7mg
Potassium 1176mg

3. Smoky Wrap Chicken Breasts
Preparation Time: 2 hours
Cooking Time: 3 hours
Servings: 6
Ingredients:

- 6 chicken breasts, skinless and boneless
- 18 bacon slices
- 3 tbsp chicken rub
- For brine:
- 1/4 cup brown sugar
- 1/4 cup kosher salt
- 4 cups water

Directions:

1. Combine together all brine ingredients into the glass dish.
2. Place chicken into the dish and coat well.
3. Soak chicken about 2 hours.
4. Rinse chicken well and coat with chicken rub.
5. Wrap each chicken breast with three bacon slices.
6. Heat the smoker to 230 F/110 C using soaked wood chips.
7. Place wrapped chicken breasts into the smoker and smoke for about 3 hours or until internal temperature reaches 165 F/73 C.
8. Serve and enjoy.

Nutrition:
Calories 441
Total Fat 25.3g
Saturated Fat 8.3g
Cholesterol 128mg
Sodium 6340mg
Total Carbohydrate 6.7g
Dietary Fiber 0g
Protein 46.1g
Vitamin D 0mcg
Calcium 19mg
Iron 2mg
Potassium 333mg

4. American Style Chicken Thighs
Preparation Time: 15 minutes
Cooking Time: 2 hours
Servings: 6
Ingredients:

- 6 (6-ounce) skinless, boneless, chicken thighs
- 6 cups water
- 1 (12-ounce) can beer
- ¼ cup brown sugar
- ¼ cup kosher salt

For Rub

- 2 tbsp brown sugar

- 2 tbsp cornstarch
- ½ tsp cayenne pepper
- Salt and freshly ground black pepper

Directions:

1. In a large bowl, add water, beer, brown sugar and salt and mix until sugar is dissolved.
2. Add the chicken thighs and mix well.
3. Cover and refrigerate overnight.
4. Remove the chicken thighs from brine ad with paper towels, pat them dry.
5. Heat the smoker to 180 degrees F.
6. For rub: in a bowl, mix together all ingredients.
7. Rub the chicken with the mixture generously.
8. Place the chicken thighs into the smoker and cook for about 1 hour.
9. Now, set the temperature of smoker to 350 degrees F and cook for about ¾-1 hour

Nutrition:

Energy 178 kcal Carbohydrate12.54 g
Calcium, Ca129 mg
Magnesium, Mg19 mg
Phosphorus, P133 mg
Iron, Fe0.48 mg
Potassium, K148 mg

5. Smoked Chicken Cutlets In Strawberries - Balsamic Marinade

Preparation Time: 2 hours
Cooking Time: 2 hours 15 minutes
Servings: 6
Ingredients:

- 3 Tbsp balsamic vinegar
- 20 medium strawberries
- 1/4 cup Extra-virgin olive oil
- 2 Tbsp chopped fresh basil
- Kosher salt and freshly ground black pepper
- 2 lbs boneless, skinless chicken breast cutlets

Directions:

1. Whisk balsamic vinegar, strawberries, olive oil and fresh basil in your blender.

2. Sprinkle marinade on and rub into the tops, bottoms, and sides of the chicken cutlets.
3. Refrigerate for 2 hours.
4. Heat Electric Smoker. Allow the smoker temperature to reach 225 degrees Fahrenheit.
5. When it is ready, add some water to the removable pan that is usually on the bottom shelf.
6. Fill the side "drawer" with dry wood chips.
7. Smoke chicken for about two hours or until the internal temperature reaches 165°F.
8. Serve hot.

Nutrition:

Calories 127
Total Fat 9g
Saturated Fat 1.2g
Cholesterol 22mg
Sodium 26mg
Total Carbohydrate 3.2g
Dietary Fiber 0.8g
Total Sugars 2g
Protein 9g
Vitamin D 0mcg
Calcium 15mg
Iron 0mg
Potassium 69mg

6. Beer Can Chicken

Preparation Time: 5 minutes
Cooking Time: 3 – 4 hours
Servings: 4
Ingredients:

- 1 can (12 ounces) beer
- 2 tablespoons apple cider vinegar
- 2 garlic cloves (minced)
- 1 whole chicken (4 to 5 pounds)
- 1 to 2 teaspoons chili powder
- 1 teaspoon salt
- 1 teaspoon onion powder
- 1/2 teaspoon freshly ground black pepper

Directions:

1. Pour 2 cups water into the smoker's water pan. Place oak or pecan wood chips in the smoker's wood tray and Heat smoker to 225°F.

2. Drink half of the can of beer. Pop two more holes in the top of the can with a can opener. Add apple cider vinegar and garlic to beer and set aside until beer comes to room temperature.

3. Remove gizzards and neck from chicken cavity if necessary. Rinse chicken inside and out with cold water and pat dry with paper towels. Mix chili powder, salt, onion powder and pepper and rub over inside and outside of chicken.

4. Set the beer can on a sturdy surface and slide the chicken cavity over the can so the chicken is standing up. Transfer chicken with can onto smoker grate and smoke until the internal temperature of the meat reaches 165°F, 3 to 4 hours. Add wood chips to the wood tray as necessary.

5. Remove chicken from smoker and remove can. Cover chicken loosely with aluminum foil and let rest for about 10 minutes. Carve chicken as desired, serve and enjoy!

Nutrition:
Calories 116
Total Fat 2.8g
Saturated Fat 0.8g
Cholesterol 32mg
Sodium 624mg
Total Carbohydrate 4.7g
Dietary Fiber 0.4g
Total Sugars 0.3g
Protein 11.2g
Vitamin D 0mcg
Calcium 18mg
Iron 1mg
Potassium 146mg

7. Herbed and Smoked Chicken
Preparation Time: 3 hours
Cooking Time: 1 hour 30 minutes
Servings: 3
Ingredients:
- 15 cups filtered water
- 4 cups nonalcoholic beer
- Salt, to taste
- 1 cup brown sugar
- 1 tablespoon rosemary
- 1 teaspoon sage
- 2 pounds whole chicken, trimmed and giblets removed
- 4 tablespoons butter
- 3 tablespoons olive oil, for basting
- 1 cup Italian seasoning
- 2 tablespoons garlic powder
- Zest of 3 small lemons

Directions:
1. Add water to a large cooking pot, then add salt and sugar.
2. Let it boil until dissolved.
3. Add the herbs and let it cook for a few minutes until aromatic.
4. Pour in the beer and then immerse chicken in it.
5. Let it refrigerate for a few hours.
6. Remove the chicken from the brine then dry with a paper towel.
7. Uncover and let it sit for one more hour in room temperate.
8. Next, butter the chicken.
9. Massage the chicken for fine coating.
10. Next, rub the chicken with Italian seasoning, garlic powder, and lemon zest.
11. Load electric smoker with the wood chips, and Heat to 250 degrees F until smoke starts to build.
12. Then, slow roast it for 1.5 hours to 2 hours, and keep basting with olive oil every 30 minutes.
13. Once the internal temperature reaches 165F and juices run clear, serve and enjoy.

Nutrition:
Calories 1284 Total Fat 74.2g
Saturated Fat 21.5g
Cholesterol 362mg
Sodium 461mg 20%
Total Carbohydrate 65g
Dietary Fiber 1g
Total Sugars 53.6g
Protein 88.6g
Calcium 119mg
Iron 5mg
Potassium 861mg

8. Smoked Chicken Thighs

Preparation Time: 2 hours 10 minutes
Cooking Time: 90 minutes
Servings: 2
Ingredients:

- 2 pounds chicken thighs
- 6 tablespoons soy sauce
- 3 teaspoons sesame oil
- 4 garlic cloves
- 4 scallions
- 1 tablespoon thyme
- 1 teaspoon allspice
- 1/3 teaspoon cinnamon
- 1/3 teaspoon crushed red pepper

Directions:

1. Combine soy sauce and oil in a bowl and rub it gently over the chicken thighs.
2. In a food processor, blend together garlic, scallion, thyme, cinnamon, allspice, and red pepper.
3. Blend it until smooth.
4. Rub it all over the thighs and seal the chick in the zip-lock plastic bag.
5. Let it marinate for about 2 hours.
6. Heat smoker to 250 degrees F, by adding the cherry wood to the smoker, and let wait for the smoke to release.
7. Smoke the chicken for 90 minutes.
8. Adjust the thermometer to read the internal temperate.
9. Once the internal temperature reaches 165F.
10. Serve it and enjoy.

Nutrition:
Calories 974
Total Fat 40.8g
Saturated Fat 10.3g
Cholesterol 404mg
Sodium 3103mg
Total Carbohydrate 9.9g
Dietary Fiber 2.3g
Total Sugars 1.6g
Protein 135.4g
Calcium 146mg
Iron 9mg
Potassium 1342mg

9. BBQ Chicken Wings Recipe

Preparation Time: 2 hours
Cooking Time: 2 hours
Servings: 4
Ingredients:

- 4 pounds turkey wings
- 1 cup of BBQ sauce

Directions:

1. Cut the chicken wings and discard the tips.
2. Marinate the wings in the BBQ sauce for about 2 hours.
3. Now Heat the smoker for a few minutes at 250 degrees F.
4. Add the cherry wood chip to the smoker and let the smoker release smoke.
5. Place the chicken into the smoker.
6. Cook for 2 hours until the internal temperature reaches 165F.
7. Use the digital meat thermometer to measure the temperature.
8. Serve and enjoy.

Nutrition:
Calories 276 Total Fat 10.2g
Saturated Fat 0g Cholesterol 0mg
Sodium 699mg Total Carbohydrate 22.7g
Dietary Fiber 0.4g Total Sugars 16.3g
Protein 23g Calcium 8mg
Iron 0mg Potassium 130mg

10. Lemon Garlic Chicken Breast Recipe

Preparation Time: 2 hours
Cooking Time: 90 minutes
Servings: 2
Ingredients:

- 2-pound chicken breasts, boneless and skinless

- 4 cloves minced garlic
- 2-inches ginger, minced
- 4 lemons, juice only
- 4 tablespoons olive oil
- Salt, to taste
- Black pepper, to taste
- 1 teaspoon turmeric

Directions:
1. Take a bowl and combine salt, pepper, lemon juice, olive oil, turmeric, ginger, and garlic in a bowl.
2. Mix well and rub the chicken with the prepared mix.
3. Let the chicken marinate for 2 hours in the refrigerator.
4. Now Heat the smoker to 250 degrees F.
5. Add the cherry wood chip to the smoker and let the smoke release.
6. Place the chicken into the smoker.
7. Cook for 90 minutes until the internal temperature reaches 165F.
8. Use the digital meat thermometer to measure the temperature.
9. Serve and enjoy.

Nutrition:
Calories 1155
Total Fat 62.2g
Saturated Fat 13.4g
Cholesterol 404mg
Sodium 472mg
Total Carbohydrate 14.8g
Dietary Fiber 3.9g
Total Sugars 3.1g
Protein 133.1g
Calcium 113mg
Iron 7mg
Potassium 1339mg

11. Authentic Citrus Smoked Chicken

Preparation Time: 15 minutes
Cooking Time: 18 hours 5 minutes
Servings: 12
Ingredients:
- 1 whole chicken
- 4 cups of lemon-lime flavored carbonated beverage

- 1 tablespoon of garlic powder
- 2 cups of soaked wood chips

Directions:
1. Transfer the whole chicken to a large sized zip bag
2. Sprinkle garlic powder and pour lemon-lime soda mix into the bag
3. Seal the bag then allow it to marinate overnight
4. Pre-heat your electric smoker to 225 degree Fahrenheit
5. Take off the chicken from the bag and transfer to your smoker rack
6. Discard the marinade
7. Smoker for 10 hours, making sure keep adding more wood chips after every hour
8. Serve and enjoy!

Nutrition:
Calories: 644
Fats: 34g
Carbs: 19g
Fiber: 0.1g

12. Amazing Mesquite Maple And Bacon Chicken

Preparation Time: 20 minutes
Cooking Time: 2 hours
Servings: 7
Ingredients:
- 4 boneless and skinless chicken breast
- Salt as needed
- Freshly ground black pepper
- 12 slices of uncooked bacon
- 1 cup of maple syrup
- ½ a cup of melted butter
- 1 teaspoon of liquid smoke

Directions:
1. Pre-heat your smoker to 250 degree Fahrenheit
2. Season the chicken with pepper and salt
3. Wrap the breast with 3 bacon slices and cover the entire surface
4. Secure the bacon with tooth picks
5. Take a medium sized bowl and stir in maple syrup, butter, liquid smoker and mix well

6. Reserve 1/3rd of this mixture for later use
7. Submerge the chicken breast into the butter mix and coat them well
8. Place a pan in your smoker and transfer the chicken to your smoker
9. Smoker for 1 to 1 and a ½ hours
10. Brush the chicken with reserved butter and smoke for 30 minutes more until the internal temperature reaches 165 degree Fahrenheit
11. Enjoy!

Nutrition:
Calories: 458
Fats: 20g
Carbs: 65g
Fiber: 1g

13. Smoked Paprika Chicken

Preparation Time: 20 minutes
Cooking Time: 2-4 hours
Servings: 4
Ingredients:
- 4-6 chicken breast
- 4 tablespoon of olive oil
- 2 tablespoon of smoked paprika
- ½ a tablespoon of kosher salt
- ¼ teaspoon of ground black pepper
- 2 teaspoon of garlic powder
- 2 teaspoon of garlic salt
- 2 teaspoon of black pepper
- 1 teaspoon of cayenne pepper
- 1 teaspoon of rosemary

Directions:
1. Pre-heat your smoker to 220 degree Fahrenheit using your favorite wood chips
2. Prepare the chicken breast according to your desired shapes

and transfer to a greased baking dish
3. Take a medium bowl and add spices, stir well
4. Press the spice mix over chicken and transfer the chicken to smoker
5. Smoke for 1-1 and a ½ hours
6. Turn-over and cook for 30 minutes more
7. Once the internal temperature reaches 165F
8. Remove from the smoker and cover with foil
9. Rest for 15 minutes
10. Enjoy!

Nutrition:
Calories: 237
Fats: 6.1g
Carbs: 14g
Fiber: 3g

14. Fully Smoked Herbal Chicken

Preparation Time: 10 minutes
Cooking Time: 60 minutes
Servings: 8
Ingredients:
- 4-6 chicken breast
- 2 tablespoon of olive oil
- Salt as needed
- Freshly ground black pepper
- 1 pack of dry Hidden Valley Ranch dressing (or your preferred one)
- ½ a cup of melted butter

Directions:
1. Pre-heat your smoker to 225 degree Fahrenheit using hickory wood
2. Season the chicken with olive oil and season with salt and pepper
3. Place the in your smoker and smoke for 1 hour
4. Take a small bowl and add ranch dressing mix and melted butter
5. After the first 30 minutes of cooking, brush the chicken with the ranch mix
6. Repeat again at the end of the cook time

7. Once the internal temperature of the chicken reaches 145 degree Fahrenheit, they are ready!

Nutrition:
Calories: 209
Fats: 13g
Carbs: 0g
Fiber: 3g

15. Orange Crispy Chicken
Preparation Time: 8 hours 30 minutes
Cooking Time: 2 hours
Servings: 4
Ingredients:
For Poultry Spice Rub
- 4 teaspoon of paprika
- 1 tablespoon of chili powder
- 2 teaspoon of ground cumin
- 2 teaspoon of dried thyme
- 2 teaspoon of salt
- 2 teaspoon of garlic powder
- 1 teaspoon of freshly ground black pepper

For The Marinade
- 4 chicken quarters
- 2 cups of frozen orange-juice concentrate
- ½ a cup of soy sauce
- 1 tablespoon of garlic powder

Directions:
1. Take a small bowl and add paprika, chili powder, cumin, salt, thyme, garlic powder, pepper and mix well
2. Transfer the chicken quarters to a large dish
3. Take a medium bowl and whisk in orange-juice concentrate, soy sauce, garlic powder, half of the spice-rub mix
4. Place the marinade over the chicken then cover
5. Refrigerate for 8 hours
6. Pre-heat your smoker to 275 degree Fahrenheit
7. Discard the marinade and rub the surface of the chicken with remaining spice rub
8. Transfer the chicken to smoker and smoker for 1 and a ½ to 2 hours

9. Remove the chicken form the smoker and check using a digital temperature that the internal temperature is 160 degree Fahrenheit
10. Allow it to rest for 10 minutes
11. Enjoy!

Nutrition:
Calories: 165
Fats: 8g
Carbs: 14g
Fiber: 2g

16. Standing Smoked Chicken
Preparation Time: 15 minutes
Cooking Time: 2 hours
Servings: 4
Ingredients:
- 12 garlic cloves, minced
- 3 whole onions, quartered
- ½ of a quartered lemon
- 1 tablespoon of salt
- 1 teaspoon of black pepper
- 1 and a ½ tablespoon of ground sage
- 1 and a ½ tablespoon of dried thyme
- 1 and a ½ tablespoon of dried rosemary
- 1 teaspoon of paprika
- 1 whole chicken of 4-6 pounds
- 3 tablespoon of vegetable oil

Directions:
1. Remove one or two of the top racks from the smoker to make room for your standing chicken
2. Smash 8 pieces of garlic cloves and add them into the water pan alongside the onion and lemon pieces
3. Pre-heat your smoker to temperature of 250 degree Fahrenheit
4. Finely mince up the rest of the 4 garlic cloves and combine them in a small sized bowl with sage, rosemary, thyme, pepper, salt, paprika and set it aside for later use

5. Remove the innards from the chicken then rinse up the bird finely
6. Pat it dry and rub it up with oil and then with the seasoning mixture created previously
7. Set your chicken in a vertical position on top of your smoker and add in just a handful of soaked chips in the chip loading area
8. Keep adding the chips for every 30 minutes
9. The chicken should be done after about 2 hours when the internal temperature registers 165 degree Fahrenheit
10. Let it cool for 15 minutes and serve

Nutrition:
Calories: 128
Fats: 3g
Carbs: 12g
Fiber: 1g

17. Smoked Chicken Salad Sandwiches
Preparation Time: 1 hour
Cooking Time: 6 hours
Servings: 8
Ingredients:
- 8 soft hoagie buns
- 3 large chicken breasts, boneless, skinless
- 3/4 cup pecans, very coarsely chopped
- 3 bay leaves
- 2 tsp. meat tenderizer
- 1/4 tsp. kosher salt
- 1/4 tsp. Cajun seasoning
- 1/4 cup butter, melted
- 1 cup finely chopped celery
- 1 1/3 cups mayonnaise
- 1 (5-oz.) bag dried cranberries
- 1/2 tsp. black pepper, freshly ground
- 1/2 tsp. salt
- Red leaf lettuce

Directions:
1. Heat the electric smoker to 225F. For the best result, use hickory chips.
2. Pierce the chicken with a fork and rub with the meat tenderizer.
3. Smoke the chicken breasts for 45 mins per pound or until the internal temperature reaches 165F.
4. Add melted butter to pecans in an aluminum foil pan. Season with kosher salt and mix the ingredients well. Coat the pecans thoroughly.
5. Put pecans on the top rack of the smoker for last 30 mins. of smoking the chicken breasts.
6. Remove the pecans and chicken. Let the breasts rest for a while and then chop the chicken well.
7. Combine the chicken, pecans, celery, dried cranberries, and mayonnaise. Mix well.Add Cajun seasoning, salt, and pepper — as much as desired.
8. Spread the mayonnaise mixture on the buns and add a lettuce leaf. Divide the chicken salad among the buns and put another lettuce leaf on the top.

Nutrition:
Calcium, Ca36 mg
Magnesium, Mg35 mg
Phosphorus, P53 mg
Iron, Fe0.46 mg
Potassium, K112 mg
Sodium, Na589 mg

18. Southwestern Smoker Chicken Wrap
Preparation Time: 8 hours 40 minutes
Cooking Time: 6 hours
Servings: 5
Ingredients:
Rub:
- 3 tsp. chili powder
- 2 tsp. paprika
- 1 tsp. onion powder
- 1 tsp. kosher salt
- 1 tsp. fresh ground pepper
- 3/4 tsp. cumin

- ½ tsp. cayenne pepper
- ½ tsp. coriander
- 1½ tsp. garlic powder

Wrap:
- 1 pound chicken breasts
- 5 flour tortillas
- 2 tomatoes, diced
- 1 onion, diced
- 2 tsp. olive oil
- 1 red bell pepper, halved
- 1 green bell pepper, halved
- Lettuce

Directions:
1. Mix all rub ingredients in a medium bowl. Coat the chicken breasts with the rub and refrigerate for 8 hrs.
2. Heat the electric smoker to 275F.
3. Put chicken breasts, bell peppers, and onion on the middle rack of the smoker.
4. Smoke the chicken breasts until the internal temperature reaches 160°F. Remove the chicken and let it cool.
5. Slice the chicken breasts. Mix chicken breasts together with lettuce, tomatoes, peppers, and onions. Divide this mixture between the tortillas.

Nutrition:
Calcium, Ca80 mg
Magnesium, Mg37 mg
Phosphorus, P218 m
Iron, Fe2.47 mg
Potassium, K396 m
Sodium, Na661 mg
Zinc, Zn1 mg
Copper, Cu0.139 mg

19. Dadgum Good Gumbo
Preparation Time: 1 hour
Cooking Time: 4 hours
Servings: 5
Ingredients:
- 4 pounds roaster chicken, cut into pieces (wings, legs, etc.)
- 2 tbsp. extra-virgin olive oil, divided
- 2 tsp. garlic, minced

- 2 packages (5 oz. each) Louisiana fish fry gumbo mix
- 1 tsp. liquid shrimp boil
- 1 pound turkey sausage
- 1 cup uncooked rice
- 1 cup celery, sliced
- 1¾ cups okra, sliced
- ½ cup sweet onion, chopped
- ½ tbsp. meat tenderizer, divided
- ½ cup green onions, thinly sliced
- French bread or crackers

Directions:
1. Heat the electric smoker to 250F.
2. Punch through each piece of chicken with a fork. Sprinkle each with 1 tbsp. olive oil and ¼ tsp. meat tenderizer. Smoke on the middle rack for 2 to 3½ hrs., till the internal temperature reaches 165°F.
3. In a large stockpot, prepare the gumbo mix, following the package directions. Add celery, okra, garlic, green onions, sweet onion and liquid shrimp boil, mixing well. Boil then simmer for 15 mins., covered. Leave it to cool.
4. Cut 1/4-inch thick slices of turkey sausage.
5. When chicken is cooked, let it rest and pull meat from bone. Combine it with sausage slices, and gumbo mixture and simmer on low for 20 mins.
6. Then add rice, mix all well and simmer for additional 15 mins. Leave pot covered, turn the heat off and let stand until rice is ready.
7. Serve with bread or crackers.

Nutrition:
Calcium, Ca139 mg
Magnesium, Mg311 mg
Phosphorus, P1151 mg
Iron, Fe9.68 mg
Potassium, K1470 mg
Sodium, Na1020 mg
Zinc, Zn9.76 mg

20. Equally Worthy Cinnamon Cured Smoked Chicken

Preparation Time: 1 hour 15 minutes
Cooking Time: 1 hour 30 minutes
Servings: 4
Ingredients:

- 1 quart of water
- ¼ cup of salt
- ¼ cup of firmly packed brown sugar
- 4 chicken breast
- 1 sliced onion
- 1 sliced lemon
- 2 halved cinnamon stick
- 1 tablespoon of ground cinnamon
- 1 tablespoon of red pepper flakes
- 1 tablespoon of seasoned salt

Directions:

1. Take a large bowl and stir in water, brown sugar and salt. Keep stirring until dissolved well
2. Add chicken, lemon, onion and cinnamon stick to the bowl and cover with plastic wrap
3. Allow it to chill for 1 hour
4. Pre-heat your smoker to 250 degree Fahrenheit with your desired wood
5. Remove the chicken and discard marinade
6. Sprinkle chicken with cinnamon, pepper flakes and seasoning salt
7. Transfer to your smoker rack and smoke for 1 and a ½ hours until the internal temperature reaches 165 degree Fahrenheit
8. Take it out and serve!

Nutrition:
Calories: 240
Fats: 5g
Carbs: 2g
Fiber: 1g

21. Smoked Chicken Tenders
Preparation Time: 8 hours 20 minutes
Cooking Time: 1 hour
Servings: 4
Ingredients:

- 4 lbs. chicken tenders, rinsed and patted dry
- 2 tsp. minced garlic
- 1½ tbsp. sesame seeds
- ¾ tsp. ginger root, peeled, freshly grated.
- ½ cup vegetable oil
- ½ cup soy sauce
- ¼ tsp. Cajun seasoning
- ¼ cup water
- Jane's Krazy Mixed-Up Salt

Directions:

1. Put soy sauce, vegetable oil, water, sesame seeds, garlic, ginger, Cajun seasoning and ½ teaspoon Jane's Krazy Salt in a bowl and mix all these ingredients well to make the marinade.
2. Place the chicken tenders in a plastic bag and add the prepared marinade. Seal the bag.
3. Place the meat in refrigerator for about 8 hrs. Make sure that the chicken is well marinated. Turn the plastic bag several times.
4. Heat the electric smoker to 250F.
5. Remove the tenders from the bag then clean the meat of any clinging marinade. Smoke for 50 mins. to 1 hr. on the middle rack. The internal temperature should reach 160F.

Nutrition:
Calcium, Ca77 mg Phosphorus, P1041 mg Iron, Fe5.09 mg Magnesium, Mg145 mg Zinc, Zn3.99 mg Potassium, K1125 mg Sodium, Na2519 mg

22. Blue Cheese Wings
Preparation Time: 10 minutes
Cooking Time: 1 hour 45 minutes
Servings: 8
Ingredients:

- 5 lb. raw chicken wings
- Pepper & Celery salt to taste

- Sauce Ingredients:
- 2 c. blue cheese chunky dressing
- ½ c. molasses
- 1 c. hot sauce
- 2 tbsp. of each:
- Minced garlic
- Extra-virgin olive oil

Directions:

1. Add some flavor to the wings with the celery salt and pepper. Arrange the wings on the smoker rack. Set the temperature to 250F and cook for one hour. Meanwhile, prepare the sauce in a saucepan using the low heat setting. Whisk all of the ingredients and simmer for 15 minutes.
2. Take the chicken from the cooker and add to a disposable aluminum pan. Empty the blue cheese sauce over the wings and place back in the cooker for 30 minutes. Serve hot and enjoy!

Nutrition:
Calories: 331Protein: 8.6g
Carbs: 3.7g Fat: 7.2g

23. Smoked Spicy Pulled Chicken

Preparation Time: 25 minutes
Cooking Time: 3 hour 30 minutes
Servings: 10
Ingredients:

- 5 lbs. Boneless chicken
- ¾ c. Butter
- ½ c. Chili powder
- ½ c. Brown sugar
- ½ tbsp. Salt
- 2 tbsps. Black pepper
- 2½ tbsps. Mustard
- 2½ tbsps. Cumin
- 1½ tbsps. Garlic powder
- ¾ tbsps. Onion powder
- ¾ tbsp. Paprika
- ¾ tsp. Cayenne pepper

Directions:

1. Heat an electric smoker to 230°F (110°C). Add apple wood chips to the smoker.
2. Place butter in a mixing bowl, using a hand mixer whisk it until softened.
3. Add chili powder, brown sugar, salt, black pepper, mustard, cumin, garlic powder, onion powder, paprika, and cayenne pepper in the bowl then continue whisking until combined.
4. Brush all sides of the chicken with the mixture then wrap with aluminum foil.
5. Place your chicken in the smoker and smoke for 3 hours.
6. Check the internal temperature and when it has reached 165°F (74°C) take the smoked chicken out from the smoker.
7. Unwrap the chicken then return it back to the smoker.
8. Smoke the chicken for about 30 minutes until brown.
9. Once ready, remove from the smoker then place on a flat surface.
10. Shred the chicken then transfer to a serving dish.
11. Enjoy.

Nutrition:
Calories: 243 Total fat: 3g Net carbs: 17g
Protein: 27g

24. Simple Buttery Smoky Chicken

Preparation Time: 20 minutes
Cooking Time: 3 hours
Servings: 10
Ingredients:

- 5 lbs. Whole Chicken
- 4 tbsps. Salt
- ½ c. Butter

Directions:

1. Rub the chicken with salt then let it sit for an hour.
2. Meanwhile, Heat the electric smoker to 250°F (120°C).
3. After an hour, rinse the chicken then pat dry using paper towels.
4. Melt the butter then brush the chicken with the melted butter.
5. Wrap the chicken with aluminum foil then place in the electric smoker.
6. Cook the chicken for 3 hours then take it out from the smoker.
7. Unwrap the chicken then cook again without cover for approximately 3 hours or until the internal temperature has reached 165°F (74°C).
8. Once it is done, remove from the electric smoker then let it sit until warm.
9. Slice the smoked chicken and serve.
10. Enjoy.

Nutrition:
Calories: 469
Total fat: 31g
Net carbs: 9.8g
Protein: 37g

25. Sweet Smoked Chicken Wings with Cinnamon
Preparation Time: 12 hours 20 minutes
Cooking Time: 2 hours
Servings: 4
Ingredients:

- 4 lbs. Chicken Wings
- 1¼ c. Brown sugar
- ½ c. Salt
- 1½ tsps. Black pepper
- 2¼ tbsps. Garlic powder
- 1¾ tbsp. Cinnamon
- ¾ tbsps. Cumin
- 1¼ tbsps. Cayenne pepper
- ½ c. Almond Butter

Directions:

1. Place brown sugar, salt, black pepper, garlic powder, cinnamon, cumin, and cayenne pepper in a zipper-lock plastic bag. Stir well.
2. Take half of the spice mixture then place in a container with a lid. Store in the refrigerator.
3. Add the chicken wings to the plastic bag then shake to season the chicken wings.
4. Place the chicken wings in the refrigerator for overnight or more—maximum 12 hours.
5. Heat an electric smoker to 200°F (93°C).
6. Remove the chicken wings from the plastic bag then transfer to a disposable aluminum pan.
7. Once the electric smoker has reached 200°F (93°C) place the pan in the smoker then smoke for 2 hours.
8. After 2 hours, take the pan out then brush the chicken wings with almond butter.
9. Sprinkle the remaining spice mixture then return the pan back to the smoker.
10. Smoke the chicken for an hour or until the internal temperature is already 165°F (73°C).
11. Take the chicken wings out from the smoker and transfer to a serving dish.
12. Serve and enjoy warm.

Nutrition:
Calories: 356
Total fat: 22.7g
Net carbs: 18g
Protein: 71.2g

26. Smoked Chicken Barbecue
Preparation Time: 20 minutes
Cooking Time: 1 hour
Servings: 5
Ingredients:

- 2½ lbs. chicken fillet
- 4 c. Barbecue sauce
- 2 tsps. Pepper
- 1 tsp. Salt

Directions:

1. Heat the electric smoker to 200°F (93°C). Pour beer into the water pan then place in the smoker.
2. Cut the chicken fillet into thick slices then place in a disposable aluminum pan.
3. Sprinkle pepper and salt over the chicken then pour barbecue sauce into the pan.
4. Place the pan in the smoker then smoke the chicken for an hour.
5. When the internal temperature has reached 165°F (74°C), remove the pan then transfer the smoked chicken to a serving dish.
6. Place the sauce over the smoked chicken then serve.
7. Enjoy.

Nutrition:

Total fat: 13g
Calories: 270
Net carbs: 0g
Protein: 78g

27. Crispy Chicken Legs and Thighs

Preparation Time: 1 hour and 30 minutes
Cooking Time: 2 hours
Servings: 6
Ingredients:

- 3 lbs. chicken legs, thigh, and legs separated
- 6 tbsps. Poultry seasoning
- 4 tbsps. Olive oil

Directions:

1. In a re-sealable plastic bag, put the chicken thighs and legs. Add the poultry seasoning, zip and thoroughly shake to make sure all the pieces are sufficiently coated and allow them to sit for 1 hour and 30 minutes
2. Heat your electric smoker to 250F.
3. Smoke the chicken for 2 hours
4. Heat the boiler on high and place the chicken. Make sure that the skin side is facing up
5. Remove from the boiler once the skin starts to crackle.

6. Serve with rice

Nutrition:

Net carbs: 1.5g
Calories: 261
Total fat: 21g
Protein: 16g

28. Whole chicken with lemon

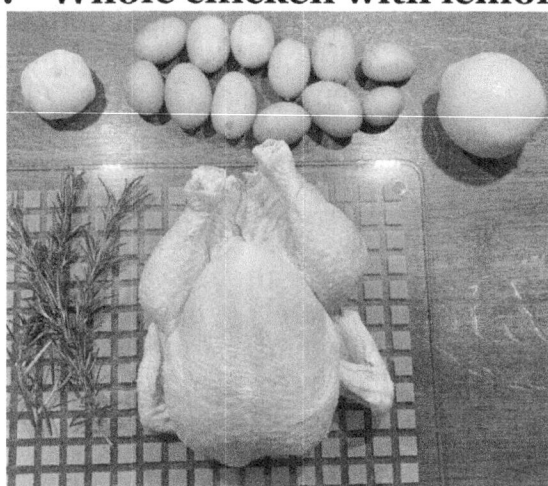

Preparation Time: 24 minutes
Cooking Time: 3 hours
Servings: 10
Ingredients:

- 3 lemon, quartered
- 3 garlic cloves
- Rosemary, parsley, and sprigs of thyme
- 3 tbsps. Butter
- 1 whole chicken
- 2 tbsps. ground sage
- 2 tbsps. fresh thyme
- 2 tbsps. Kosher salt
- 2 tbsps. Fresh rosemary

Directions:

1. Heat your smoker to 250°F.
2. Fill the chicken using the stuffing ingredients
3. Combine the rubbing ingredients then rub on the chicken evenly
4. Using indirect heat, smoke the chicken for 3 hours and remove.
5. Rest for 10 minutes and serve.

Nutrition:

Calories: 331
Total fat: 13g
Net carbs: 27g
Protein: 27g

29. Fruits and Nut Stuffed Chicken Breast

Preparation Time: 9 hours
Cooking Time: 3 hours
Servings: 4
Ingredients:
- 4 skinless chicken breasts
- 12 oz. Apple-cherry concentrate
- ¾ c. red wine vinegar
- 1 tbsp. ground cinnamon
- ½ c. diced apple
- ½ c. diced cherries
- ½ c. chopped cranberries
- ½ c. walnuts

Directions:
1. Create a pocket into each chicken breast
2. Put the breasts in a re-sealable plastic bag
3. Mix the marinade ingredients and place them in a microwave for 15 sec
4. Pour the marinade mixture into the plastic bags, seal and refrigerate for 9 hours
5. After refrigeration, combine the stuffing ingredients in a bowl. Stuff the breasts and tie with a butcher twine
6. Heat your electric smoker until temperatures reach 250°F.
7. Place the breasts on the rack and maintain the same temperature.
8. Smoke for 3 hours
9. Allow to rest for few minutes and serve

Nutrition:
Calories: 579
Total fat: 41.6g
Net carbs: 7.6g
Protein: 44.3g

30. Electric Smoker Chicken Breast Sandwich

Preparation Time: 2 hours 40 minutes
Cooking Time: 3 hours
Servings: 3
Ingredients:
- 3 Pieces chicken breasts
- 16 c. water
- ½ tbsp. sea salt
- 4 tbsps. Olive oil
- ½ c. soy sauce
- ½ c. sugar
- Crushed garlic cloves
- Pepper cones
- A handful of spinach

Directions:
1. Remove fat from the chicken breast and clean in cold water.
2. To make the chicken juicer and tender brine it by adding sea salt and water into a bowl then stir until the salt dissolves.
3. Place the chicken breasts in a plastic bag full of brine.
4. Extract out the excess air, seal and refrigerate for 2 hours.
5. Drain the breasts and dry with a paper towel after 2 hours and leave to air dry for 40 minutes.
6. Heat the electric smoker to 250° F.
7. Put the breasts on the grill and cook for 60 minutes.
8. Check the meat temperature after 60 minutes and wait for 45 more minutes before checking again.
9. After the breasts are at the temperature of 165° F, pull them out of the smoker.
10. Place the breasts on aluminum foil and let them cool for 12 minutes at room temperature.
11. Add lettuce, tomatoes, and sandwich the breasts in between the slices of bread.
12. Enjoy.

Nutrition:
Calories: 115
Total fat: 1.1g
Net carbs: 0.1g
Protein: 25g

31. Sweet Chili Chicken Wings

Preparation Time: 2 hours
Cooking Time: 3 hours 30 minutes
Servings: 4
Ingredients:
- 5 lbs. chicken wings

- 3 tbsps. Black pepper
- 2 tbsps. Onion powder
- 2 tbsps. Chili powder
- 2 tbsps. Garlic powder
- 2 tbsps. Salt
- 1½ c. honey
- ½ c. spicy barbecue sauce
- 4 tbsps. Apple juice

Directions:
1. Heat the smoker to 225°F.
2. Prepare 2 aluminum baking sheets.
3. Mix all the ingredients for the rub.
4. Divide wings and rub among 2 re-sealable plastic bags. Seal the bags then shake well until the pieces are evenly coated.
5. Refrigerate for 2 hours.
6. In the meantime place your wood chips in the smoker.
7. Remove marinated wings from the bags and transfer them to the baking sheets, one portion of each sheet.
8. Place the pans in the smoker, and cook for 3 hours, turning once after the first 2 hours.
9. Meanwhile, combine sauce ingredients in a saucepan over medium heat until heated through.
10. Coat wings evenly with sauce, and return to smoker for 30 more mins.

Nutrition:
Protein: 6.4g
Calories: 42
Total fat: 1.7g
Net carbs: 0g

CHAPTER 5:

Pork Recipes

32. Smoked Pork Ribs

Preparation Time: 30 minutes
Cooking Time: 6 hours
Servings: 4
Ingredients:
Rub:

- 1/4 cup ancho chili powder
- 2 tsp. Spanish paprika
- 2 tsp. freshly ground black pepper
- 2 tsp. dry mustard
- 2 tsp. kosher salt
- 2 tsp. ground coriander
- 1 tbsp. dried oregano
- 1 tbsp. ground cumin
- 2 tsp. chile de arbol
- 2 racks St. Louis-style pork ribs, 12 ribs each, membrane removed
- 1/4 cup canola oil

Mop Mixture:

- 2 cups cider vinegar
- 2 tsp. light brown sugar
- 1/2 tbsp. cayenne powder
- Few dashes hot pepper sauce (recommended: Tabasco)
- 1 tbsp. kosher salt
- 1/4 tbsp. freshly ground black pepper
- 1 quart apple cider

Directions:

1. Get a small bowl, and combine all the spices inside it. Brush each side of all the racks with a little bit of oil and your spice mixture. Wrap it all in plastic and refrigerate overnight, for 12 hours.
2. Get a large pot heated up over low heat. Add all the mop ingredients into it. You're going to want to bring it all to a simmer, and just cook it until the sugar has completely dissolved. Allow it cool at room temperature.
3. Take the rips out of the fridge one hour before it's time to start smoking them. Also, at this time put your apple cider in a heatproof pan and place it within the smoker.
4. Place your ribs on the rack in the smoker. Once every hour for the first five hours you're going to brush your ribs with the mop. On the last hour, brush your ribs with the barbecue sauce every 10 minutes.
5. Afterwards, take your ribs off the smoking rack and serve.

Nutrition:
Calcium, Ca77 mg Magnesium, Mg51 mg
Phosphorus, P251 m Iron, Fe3.89 m
Potassium, K655 mg

33. Apple-Injected Smoked Pork
Preparation Time: 10 minutes
Cooking Time: 6 hours
Servings: 12
Ingredients:

- 2 cups apple cider
- 2 tsp. dry rub seasoning
- 2 tsp. apple cider vinegar

- 2 tsp. honey
- 1/2 tbsp. cayenne pepper
- 1/4 cup orange juice
- 1/2 cup lemon juice
- Dash Worcestershire sauce
- 2 tsp. kosher salt
- 1 (6 to 8-lb.) pork butt

Directions:
1. Whisk together all ingredients for your marinade.
2. Put your pork in a large dish. Using a syringe, inject your marinade ¾ of the way inside of the pork. You're going to want to do this several times in a different place each time on your eat.
3. Close the pork in plastic wrap and store in the fridge between 4-12 hours.
4. Place pork in the smoker.
5. Drain any liquid that has remained on the meat, and be sure to pat it dry. Season the pork with your dry rub seasoning so it has a better taste. You're going to want to cover both sides.
6. Cool the pork for a few minutes before serving.

Nutrition:
Calcium, Ca48 mg
Magnesium, Mg61 mg
Phosphorus, P680 mg
Iron, Fe3.26 mg
Potassium, K1336 mg
Sodium, Na894 mg
Zinc, Zn9.41 mg

34. Smoked Pork Chops
Preparation Time: 15 minutes
Cooking Time: 1 hour 10 minutes
Servings: 4
Ingredients:
- 4 tbsp. salt
- 2 tsp. freshly ground black pepper
- 2 tsp. dark brown sugar
- 2 tsp. ground thyme
- 2 tsp. onion powder
- 1 tbsp. cayenne pepper
- 4 center cut, bone-in pork chops

- Buttermilk BBQ Sauce:
- 1 cup apple cider
- 1 tbsp. brown sugar
- 1/2 preferred BBQ sauce
- 1 tbsp. buttermilk

Directions:
1. Mix together salt, onion powder, black pepper, thyme, cayenne pepper, and brown sugar.
2. After this you're going to want to rub your pork chops with this mixture. Wrap the chops in plastic wrap and store in the fridge for four hours.
3. Place your chops in the smoker.
4. Get a Saucepan and heat it up to medium-low heat.
5. Add in the brown sugar and apple cider. Stir everything together.
6. Let the mixture reduce for only 25 minutes.
7. Turn the heat down to low, and pour in your preferred barbecue sauce. Stir everything well.
8. Once the sauce has been thoroughly cooked, turn off the heat source.
9. Add in the buttermilk and stir it all together. Serve this over the pork chops, and you're done!

Nutrition:
Calcium, Ca36 mg
Magnesium, Mg39 mg
Phosphorus, P266 mg
Iron, Fe0.91 mg
Potassium, K577 mg

35. Smoked Boston Butt Roast
Preparation Time: 20 minutes
Cooking Time: 4 hours
Servings: 6
Ingredients:
- 1 (5 lb) pork butt roast
- 4 tsp. House Seasoning, recipe follows
- 2 tsp. seasoned salt
- 1 medium onion, sliced
- 1 cup water
- 3 bay leaves

- Sweet or Smoky BBQ sauce
- House Seasoning:
- 1 cup salt
- 1/4 cup black pepper
- 1/4 cup garlic powder

Directions:

1. On one side of your roast sprinkle two tsp. of the House Seasoning. Be sure to rub it in well with your fingers. Flip your roast over and rub in the remaining two tsp. of the House Seasoning. Repeat this process with your seasoned salt.
2. Place your roast on a large pan for roasting. Add in the bay leaves, onion, and water. Place the roast in your smoker for 4 hours.
3. The internal temperature for the meat should be 170 degrees. Once it is, allow it to cool for a few minutes.
1. Serve this roast with sweet or smoky BBQ sauce.

Nutrition:
Calcium, Ca31 mg
Magnesium, Mg42 mg
Phosphorus, P342 mg
Iron, Fe1.58 mg
Potassium, K596 mg

36. **Smoked Pork**
37. **Shoulder**

Preparation Time: 30 minutes
Cooking Time: 5 hours 30 minutes
Servings: 6
Ingredients:

- 1 (5-6 lb.) pork shoulder/Boston butt pork roast
- 2 tsp. salt
- Sweet BBQ Sauce

Directions:

1. Season with salt your pork shoulder. Close it up and chill it in the fridge for half an hour.
2. Place the pork inside the smoker. Close the lid.
3. Cook the meat for Five and a half hours. The temperature of your pork inside should be 165 degrees. Rotate the pork over for the last two hours of its smoking.

4. Remove the pork, give it a few minutes to cool. Serve with sweet BBQ sauce.

Nutrition:
Calcium, Ca101 mg
Magnesium, Mg89 mg
Phosphorus, P809 mg
Iron, Fe6.81 mg
Potassium, K1186 mg

Sodium, Na890 mg

38. **Smoked Pork Sausage**

Preparation Time: 60 minutes
Cooking Time: 3 hours
Servings: 30 sausage
Ingredients:

- 20 lbs of home-dressed lean pork meat
- 10 lbs of clear fat pork
- 1/2 lb fine salt (best quality)
- 2 tsp. sugar
- 1 tbsp. ginger
- 2 tsp. pepper
- 1 tbsp. sage
- 2 tsp. cure (either Instacure #1 or Prague Powder #1)

Directions:

1. Cut the meat into cubes. Grind them all together in an extra-large bowl with the spices.
2. Using a sausage grinder, pass the mixed meat and spices through a medium plate on the grinder.

3. Stuff the sausages in natural pork casings so you'll be able to smoke them.
4. Place them in the smoker.

Nutrition:
Calcium, Ca55 mg
Magnesium, Mg103 mg
Phosphorus, P1260 mg
Iron, Fe5.27 mg
Potassium, K1529 mg

39. Sweet Smoked Pork Ribs
Preparation Time: 20 minutes
Cooking Time: 4 hours
Servings: 15
Ingredients:
- 1/4 cup salt
- 1/4 cup white sugar
- 2 tsp. packed brown sugar
- 2 tsp. ground black pepper
- 2 tsp. ground white pepper
- 2 tsp. onion powder
- 1 tbsp. garlic powder
- 1 tbsp. chili powder
- 1 tbsp. paprika
- 1 tbsp. ground cumin
- 10 lbs baby back pork ribs
- 1 cup apple juice
- 1/4 cup packed brown sugar
- 1/4 cup sweet BBQ sauce

Directions:
1. Mix salt, cumin, white sugar, paprika, 2 tsp. of brown sugar, chili powder, black pepper, garlic powder, white pepper, and onion powder. Rub this mixture onto the back of the rips on all of the sides. Wrap your ribs in plastic wrap.Place the pork fridge for half an hour.
2. Start your smoker. Put your ribs on the rack.
3. Combine the barbeque sauce, apple juice, and 1/4 brown sugar. Every 30 to 45 minutes brush the ribs with the barbeque sauce for the first hour. Brush the sauce onto the rips during its last half hour of cooking.

4. When the ribs have finished, wrap them up in aluminum foil. Allow them to sit for an additional 15 minutes. You may serve them afterward.

Nutrition:
Calcium, Ca82 mg Magnesium, Mg79 mg
Phosphorus, P636 mg
Iron, Fe3.47 mg Potassium, K1141 mg
Sodium, Na2139 mg
Zinc, Zn9.26 mg

40. Smoked Pork Tenderloin
Preparation Time: 15 minutes
Cooking Time: 3 hours
Servings: 4
Ingredients:
- ½ cup sweet BBQ sauce
- 2 pork tenderloins (1.5-2 lb.s each)
- ½ cup marinade

Directions:
1. Put your pork loin in your chosen marinade. Marinade for 3 hours or overnight.
2. Drain the marinade. Place your pork loin on the rack.
3. Half an hour before taking the loin out of the smoker, pout it with barbeque sauce
4. When done smoking remove the pork loin. Pack the pork loin in some foil for ten minutes
5. Slice the pork loin thinly.

Nutrition:
Calcium, Ca29 mg Magnesium, Mg80 mg
Phosphorus, P638 mg
Iron, Fe2.97 mg
Potassium, K1105 mg
Sodium, Na930 mg
Zinc, Zn5.68 mg

41. Smoked Asian Style Pork Tenderloin
Preparation Time: 2 hours
Cooking Time: 2 hours 15 minutes
Servings: 10
Ingredients:
- 1 cup brown sugar
- 1/4 cup tamari sauce
- 1 cup Apple Cider Vinegar

- 1 tsp fresh ginger grated
- 1 tsp Salt and black pepper to taste
- 5 lbs pork tenderloin

Directions:

1. Whisk brown sugar, tamari sauce, apple cider vinegar, grated ginger and salt and pepper to taste in mixing bowl.
2. Place the tenderloin in a large container and pour apple cider mixture; toss well. Place in fridge for 4 - 5 hours (preferably overnight).
3. Heat your electric smoker to 225°F.
4. When it is ready, add some water to the removable pan that is usually on the bottom shelf.
5. Fill the side "drawer" with dry wood chips.
6. Remove tenderloin from fridge and pat dry on kitchen paper.
7. Place pork in a smoker, and smoke for 2 1/2 - 3 hours, or until internal temp reaches 150°F.
8. Take off from smoker and wrap with aluminum foil. Place back into smoker for 30 minutes, or until internal temp reaches 145°F.
9. When ready let cool for 15 minutes before slicing and serving.

Nutrition:
Amount Per Serving
Calories 294,47
Calories From Fat 44Total Fat 4,94g
Saturated Fat 1,59gCholesterol 147,42mg
Sodium 335,22mgPotassium 960,75mg
Total Carbohydrates 11,32g
Fiber 0,08g Sugar 9,68g Protein 47,87g

42. Smoked Hot Pepper Pork Tenderloin

Preparation Time: 10 minutes
Cooking Time: 3 hours
Servings: 6
Ingredients:

- 3/4 cup chicken stock
- 1/2 cup tomato-basil sauce
- 2 tsp hot red chili pepper
- 1 Tbsp oregano
- Salt and pepper

- 2 lb pork tenderloin

Directions:

1. Whisk together the chicken stock, tomato-basil sauce, hot red chili pepper, oregano, and salt and pepper.
2. Brush generously all over the tenderloin.
3. Heat your electric smoker to 225°F.
4. When it is ready, add some water to the removable pan that is usually on the bottom shelf.
5. Fill the side "drawer" with dry wood chips.
6. Place meat in the smoker and smoke internal temperature of 145 degrees F, for about 2 1/2 - 3 hours.
7. Before slicing let it rest for 10 minutes.
8. Serve.

Nutrition:
Calories 360,71
Total Fat 14,32g
Saturated Fat 5,1g
Cholesterol 159,8mg
Sodium 331,83mg
Potassium 905,83mg
Total Carbohydrates 3,21g
Fiber 1,46g
Protein 52,09g
Sugar 1,01g

43. Smoked Pork Chops in Garlic Soy Marinade

Preparation Time: 1 hour
Cooking Time: 3 hours 15 minutes
Servings: 8
Ingredients:

- 1 cup soy sauce
- 1/4 cup lemon juice freshly squeezed
- 1 Tbsp brown sugar
- 5 lbs bone-in pork loin
- 3 cloves garlic minced

Directions:

1. Whisk minced garlic, soy sauce, fresh lemon juice, and brown sugar in a large resealable plastic bag: toss to combine well.

2. Place in the pork chops. Seal bag and refrigerate overnight.
3. Remove the pork chops from marinade; reserve marinade for basting.
4. Heat your electric smoker to 225°F.
5. When it is ready, add some water to the removable pan that is usually on the bottom shelf. Fill the side "drawer" with dry wood chips.
6. Arrange pork chops on racks and smoke for 3 hours.
7. After 3 hours, remove ribs, baste generously with reserved marinade and wrap in aluminum foil.
8. Return the smoker and cook for an additional 1 to 1 1/2 hours, or until internal temperature reaches 160° F.
9. Remove meat from smoker and let it rest for 10 - 15 minutes. Serve hot.

Nutrition:
Calories 554,09 Total Fat 31,35g
Saturated Fat 6,71g Potassium 1027,42mg
Total Carbohydrates 5,3g
Fiber 0,3g
Sugar 2,41g
Protein 59,24g

44. Smoked Pork Loin with Beer-Anise Marinade

Preparation Time: 30 minutes
Cooking Time: 3 hours
Servings: 6
Ingredients:
Marinade
- 1/4 cup honey
- 1 1/2 cups dark beer
- 2 tsp Anise seeds

- 1Tbs fresh thyme finely chopped
- Salt and pepper to taste

Pork
- 3 lbs pork loin

Directions:
1. In a casserole mix all the marinade ingredients.
2. Place the pork with marinade mixture in a resealable plastic bag. Refrigerate for several hours, or overnight.
3. Place the water in the pan at the bottom of your smoker. Fill the drawer or tray with wood chips.
4. Heat your smoker (use a 2-zone or Indirect setup) to about 225°F.
5. Remove the pork from marinade (reserve marinade for later) and place on kitchen towel.
6. Put the meat in the smoker then smoke till the internal temperature is 145F, about 2 1/2 to 3 hours.
7. Remove the meat then let rest for 10 minutes before slicing.
8. Serve hot or cold.

Nutrition:
Calories 360,86 Total Fat 7,92g
Saturated Fat 2,76g Cholesterol 149,69mg
Sodium 211,47mg
Potassium 917,04mg
Total Carbohydrates 14,56g
Fiber 0,4g Sugar 11,61g
Protein 51,33g

45. Smoked Pork Loin with Sweet Habanero Rub

Preparation Time: 30 minutes
Cooking Time: 3 hours
Servings: 8
Ingredients:
- 4 lbs pork loin
- Sauce
- Mandarin Habanero Seasoning or any other hot sauce
- 1 cup honey
- 1 cup mustard
- 1 Tbsp Salt and white pepper to taste

Directions:

1. Combine the Habanero seasoning, honey, mustard and tamari sauce in a mixing bowl.
2. Rub lots of spice mix all over the meat.
3. Heat your electric smoker to 225°F.
4. When it is ready, add some water to the removable pan that is usually on the bottom shelf.
5. Fill the side "drawer" with dry wood chips (hickory or maple).
6. Put meat in the smoker and smoke till the internal temperature is 145F, about 2 1/2 to 3 hours.
7. When the meat reaches a temperature around 145 degrees F, remove the meat, then cover it for about 5 to 10 minutes.
8. Slice and serve hot.

Nutrition:
Calories 429,91
Total Fat 8,4g
Saturated Fat 2,78g
Cholesterol 149,69mg
Potassium 921,88mg
Total Carbohydrates 36,36g
Fiber 0,83g
Sugar 34,93g
Protein 51,73g

46. Smoked Pork Ribs with Fresh Herbs
Preparation Time: 30 minutes
Cooking Time: 5 hours
Servings: 6
Ingredients:
- 1/2 cup olive oil
- 1 tsp fresh parsley finely chopped
- 1 tsp fresh sage finely chopped
- 1 tsp fresh rosemary finely chopped
- Salt and ground black pepper to taste
- 3 lbs. bone-in pork rib roast

Directions:
1. Combine the olive oil, garlic, parsley, sage, rosemary, salt, and pepper in a bowl; stir well.
2. Generously rub the herbs mix all over the meat.
3. Heat your electric smoker to 225°F.

4. When it is ready, add some water to the removable pan that is usually on the bottom shelf.
5. Fill the side "drawer" with dry wood chips (Hickory and mesquite).
6. Smoke the meat directly on the racks for 3 hours at 225 degrees Fahrenheit.
7. Remove the ribs from the racks and tightly wrap them in aluminum foil
8. Move them back in the smoker for 2 hours.
9. Transfer to a serving platter; let it rest 10 - 15 minutes before serving.

Nutrition:
Calories 532,35
Total Fat 40,14g
Saturated Fat 7,24g
Potassium 678,54mg
Total Carbohydrates 0,11g
Fiber 0,07g
Sugar 0g
Protein 40,65g

47. Sweet Espresso Ribs
Preparation Time: 10 minutes
Cooking Time: 6 hours
Servings: 6
Ingredients:
- 1 large rack of baby back ribs, at room temperature, membrane removed
- ½ cup brown sugar
- ½ cup ground espresso beans
- 3 tablespoons ground black pepper
- 2 tablespoons olive oil
- 2 tablespoons butter, unsalted, cubed
- BBQ sauce as needed

Directions:
1. Prepare the grill, and for this, go to Electric Smoker app, set the grill temperature to 225 degrees F, and let it heat.
2. Meanwhile, brush ribs with oil, then stir together sugar, espresso, and black pepper and sprinkle this mixture on ribs until coated on all sides.

3. When the smoker has heated, open its lid, place ribs on the grill by using a tong, shut with lid, and let it grill for 2 hours.

4. Then take a large piece of foil, place ribs on it, spread butter cubes on top, sprinkle with remaining espresso mixture, wrap the ribs and then continue grilling for 2 hours or until tender.

5. Then remove ribs from the grill, unwrap it, and spread evenly with sauce.

6. Return the ribs on the grill and then continue grilling for 1 hour or 1 hour and 30 minutes until done.

7. Rest for 15 minutes, and then serve.

Nutrition:
Calories: 416 Cal
Fat: 21 g
Carbs: 35 g
Protein: 22 g
Fiber: 1 g

48. Perfect Smoked Pork Butt
Preparation Time: 10 minutes
Cooking Time: 6 hours
Servings: 8
Ingredients:

- 6 lb. bone-in pork butt
- 1 tbsp. chili powder
- 1/2 tbsp. cayenne pepper
- 1 tbsp. paprika
- 1 tsp. garlic powder
- 1 tbsp. onion powder
- 2 tbsp. dark sugar
- Coarse salt and freshly ground pepper

Directions:

1. In a bowl, blend all ingredients together and completely rub the butt.

2. Place in the aluminum tray - uncovered - and smoke for 6 hours (1 hour per pound) at 250°F.

3. Remove from smoker then strain the juice into a small bowl.

4. Place the butt in double foil.

5. Pour juice over pork and, then wrap 4 more times.

6. Place back on the smoker at 250°F until internal temp reaches at 195°F for pulled pork.

7. Serve hot. Enjoy!

Nutrition:
Calories: 469 Fat: 35 g
Protein: 54 g Carbs: 5.6 g

49. Smoked Avocado Pork Ribs Appetizer
Preparation Time: 4 - 12 hours
Cooking Time: 4 hours 30 minutes
Servings: 7
Ingredients:

- 3 lb. spare ribs
- 1 cup avocado oil
- 1 tsp. garlic salt
- 1 tsp. garlic powder
- 1/2 tsp. onion powder
- Fresh parsley, finely chopped
- Salt and pepper, to taste

Directions:

1. In a bowl, combine avocado oil, garlic salt, garlic powder, onion powder, chopped parsley and salt and pepper.

2. Place pork ribs in a shallow container and pour avocado mixture evenly.

3. Cover then refrigerate for at least 4 hours, or overnight.

4. Remove pork ribs from marinade (reserve marinade) and smoke for 3 hours at 225°F, in the Heated smoker.

5. Remove the ribs from the smoker.

6. Baste generously with reserved marinade, and wrap in heavy-duty aluminum foil.

7. Return to smoker then cook for an additional 1 to 1 1/2 hours, or until internal temp reaches 160°F.

8. Transfer pork chops on serving plate and let rest for 15 - 20 minutes.

9. Serve hot. Enjoy!

Nutrition:
Calories: 678.8 Fat: 61.1 g
Protein: 30.2 g Carbs: 0.6 g

50. Smoked Pork Ribs with Avocado Oil

Preparation Time: 4 hours
Cooking Time: 2 hours
Servings: 7
Ingredients:

- 1 cup avocado oil
- 1 tsp garlic salt, or to taste
- 2 tsp garlic and onion powder
- 1/2 cup fresh parsley finely chopped
- 4 lbs spare ribs

Directions:

1. Whisk avocado oil, garlic salt, garlic powder, onion powder, fresh chopped parsley in a mixing bowl.
2. Put pork ribs in a shallow container and pour avocado mixture over; toss to combine well. Refrigerate for at least 4 hours, or at overnight.
3. Heat your electric smoker to 225°F.
4. When it is ready, add some water to the removable pan that is usually on the bottom shelf. Fill the side "drawer" with dry wood chips.
5. Remove pork ribs from marinade (reserve marinade) and arrange the pork chops on the rack.
6. Smoke for 1 1/2 hours at 225 degrees F.
7. Remove the ribs, baste generously with reserved marinade, and wrap in heavy-duty aluminum foil.
8. Return the meat to the smoker then cook for an additional 1 hour, or until internal temp reaches 160 degrees.
9. Transfer pork chops on serving plate and let rest for 15 - 20 minutes before serving.

Nutrition:
Calories 760,68
Total Fat 76,26g
Saturated Fat 21,32g
Cholesterol 207,36mg
Sodium 505,73mg
Potassium 661,57mg
Total Carbohydrates 1,06g
Fiber 0,37g
Sugar 0,06g Protein 40,37g

51. Beer Brats

Preparation Time: 10 minutes
Cooking Time: 3 hours
Servings: 6
Ingredients:

- 6 uncooked German brats
- 1 medium sweet onion, peeled, chopped into thick slices
- 3 tablespoons brown sugar
- 8 ounces butter, salted, cut into 8 pieces
- 22 ounces amber ale

Directions:

1. Switch on the smoker, go to the WiFi setting on your cell phone, and then connect with the grill by using your serial number as the password.
2. Prepare the grill, and for this, go to Electric Smoker app, set the smoker temperature to 250 degrees F, and let it heat.
3. Meanwhile, take a large pan, scatter onion in its bottom, sprinkle with sugar, top with butter slices and sausages, and then pour ale over the sausages.
4. When the grill has Heated, open its lid, place the pan on the grill by using a tong, shut with lid, and let it grill for 3 hours until thoroughly cooked.
5. Serve straight away.

Nutrition:
Calories: 230.4 Cal
Fat: 21 g
Carbs: 2 g
Protein: 12 g
Fiber: 0.4 g

52. Smoked Chops in Sweet Soy Marinade

Preparation Time: 10 minutes
Cooking Time: 4 hours 30 minutes
Servings: 8
Ingredients:

- 2 garlic cloves, minced
- 3/4 cup soy sauce
- 1/4 cup lemon juice, freshly squeezed
- 1 tbsp. chili sauce
- 1 tbsp. brown sugar
- 5 lb. bone-in pork loin

Directions:

1. In a large, resealable plastic bag, combine minced garlic, soy sauce, fresh lemon juice, chili sauce and brown sugar; stir.
2. Place inside the pork chops. Seal bag and refrigerate overnight.
3. Remove the pork chops from marinade; reserve marinade for basting.
4. Heat the smoker to 225°F and add wood chips.
5. Arrange the pork chops on grill and smoke for 3 hours.
6. After 3 hours, remove ribs, baste generously with reserved marinade and wrap in heavy-duty aluminum foil.
7. Return the smoker then cook for an additional 1 to 1 1/2 hours, or until internal temperature reaches 160° F.
8. Serve hot. Enjoy!

Nutrition:
Calories: 549.5
Fat: 31.4 g
Protein: 58.8 g
Carbs: 4.5 g

53. Pork Belly Burnt Ends

Preparation Time: 10 minutes
Cooking Time: 5 hours
Servings: 4
Ingredients:

- 1 Pork belly slab
- BBQ pork rub as needed
- BBQ sauce as needed

Directions:

1. Cut the pork belly into 1-inch long strips, starting from the skinless side, and then place the strips in a large bowl.
2. Add rub, toss until coated, and then let it marinate for a minimum of 30 minutes in the refrigerator.
3. Prepare the grill, and for this, go to Electric Smoker app, set the temperature to 250 degrees F, and let it Heat.
4. When the grill has Heated, open its lid, place pork belly strips on the grill by using a tong, shut with lid and let it grill for 3 to 4 hours or set the food temperature to 198 degrees F in the app and let it grill until the food reaches the set food temperature.
5. Once the app shows that the internal temperature of the pork has reached 198 degrees F, open the grill and then transfer pork strips to a cutting board.
6. Let pork cool for 15 minutes, then cut them into 1-inch cubes and place them in a disposable aluminum foil tray.
7. Add BBQ sauce, toss until well coated, cover the tray with foil, return it on the grill and continue grilling for 1 hour.
8. Serve straight away.

Nutrition:
Calories: 300 Cal
Fat: 13 g
Carbs: 21 g
Protein: 26 g
Fiber: 1 g

54. Shredded pork loin with smoked hot chili pepper

Preparation Time: 4 – 5 hours
Cooking Time: 2 hours 20 minutes
Servings: 6
Ingredients:

- 4 lb. pork loin
- 1 spring onion, finely chopped
- 1 tbsp. minced garlic
- 1/4 cup fresh lime juice
- 1/4 cup apple cider vinegar
- 2 tbsp. chipotles in adobo sauce
- 3 bay leaves
- 1 tbsp. dried oregano
- 1 tbsp. ground cumin
- 1 tbsp. kosher salt

Directions:

1. Whisk the garlic, chipotles, onion, lime juice, vinegar, bay leaves, oregano, cumin, salt in a bowl.
2. Cut the pork loin into four pieces and place in a large container; rub both sides of tenderloin with salt.
3. Pour the chipotles mixture over the pork and toss to combine well.
4. Cover and refrigerate for 4 - 5 hours or overnight.
5. Heat smoker to 225°F.
6. Remove the pork from marinade then dry with kitchen towel.
7. Smoke unwrapped for 1 1/2 hours, or until internal temp reaches 150°F.
8. Remove from the smoker and wrap with heavy-duty aluminum foil.
9. Put back into the smoker for an additional 30 minutes, or until internal temp reaches 165°F.

10. Transfer pork to the plate and let cook for 15 minutes.
11. When cool, use two forks or your fingers to shred the meat into pieces.
12. Serve and enjoy!

Nutrition:
Calories: 396.1
Fat: 10.6 g
Protein: 68.2 g
Carbs: 2.6 g

55. Rodeo Drive Baby Ribs

Preparation Time: 4 – 12 hours
Cooking Time: 3 hours
Servings: 8
Ingredients:

- 4 lb. baby ribs (without membrane)
- Salt and ground pepper
- 1 can (15 oz.) tomato sauce
- 2 tbsp. maple syrup
- 2 tbsp. apple cider vinegar
- 2 tsp. smoked paprika
- 1/2 tsp. garlic powder

Directions:

1. Cut the Baby Ribs into two-three pieces, place in a shallow container and rub with salt and pepper.
2. Combine the tomato sauce, maple syrup, apple cider vinegar, paprika, garlic and onion powder.
3. Pour sauce over spareribs evenly.
4. Refrigerate for about 4 hours or overnight.
5. Heat the smoker to 225°F then add wood chips.
6. Remove the pork chops from marinade then dry.
7. Smoke for 3 - 4 hours, or until internal temperature reaches 165°F.
8. Serve hot. Enjoy!

Nutrition:
Calories: 567.6
Fat: 53.3 g
Protein: 35.9 g
Carbs: 6.8 g

56.   Cherry Chipotle Ribs

Preparation Time: 10 minutes
Cooking Time: 6 hours
Servings: 4
Ingredients:

- 1 large rack of baby back ribs, at room temperature, membrane removed
- ½ cup brown sugar
- 2 tablespoons mustard paste
- Pork rub as needed
- 2 tablespoons butter, unsalted
- 3 tablespoons honey
- Cherry chipotle sauce as needed

Directions:

1. Prepare the grill, and for this, go to Electric Smoker app, set the temperature to 225 degrees F, and let it Heat.
2. Meanwhile, prepare the ribs, and for this, rub with mustard paste and then sprinkle with pork rub until coated on all sides.
3. When the grill has Heated, open its lid, place ribs on the grill, shut with lid, then grill for 2 hours.
4. Then take a large piece of foil, place ribs on it, spread butter and honey on top, sprinkle with sugar, wrap the ribs and then continue grilling for 2 hours or until tender.
5. Then remove ribs from the grill, unwrap it, and spread evenly with chipotle sauce.
6. Switch the temperature of the grill to 275 degrees F, return the ribs on the grill and continue grilling for 1 hour or 1 hour and 30 minutes until done.
7. Let the meat rest for 15 minutes and then serve.

Nutrition:
Calories: 292.5 Cal
Fat: 17 g
Carbs: 20 g
Protein: 13 g
Fiber: 2 g

57.   Baby Back Ribs

Preparation Time: 10 minutes
Cooking Time: 9 hours
Servings: 6
Ingredients:

- 2 racks of baby back ribs, at room temperature
- Cherry chipotle sauce as needed
- For the Marinade:
- 2 tablespoons minced garlic
- 1 teaspoon onion powder
- 2 teaspoons ground black pepper
- 1 tablespoon brown sugar
- 1 cup soy sauce
- 2 tablespoons red wine vinegar
- ¼ cup olive oil
- ½ teaspoon Tabasco sauce
- ¼ cup white wine

Directions:

1. Take a small bowl, place all the ingredients for the marinade in it and then whisk until combined.
2. Pour the marinade in a large plastic bag, add ribs, seal the bag, turn it upside down to coat ribs with the marinade and then let it marinate for a minimum of 4 hours.
3. When ready to grill, switch on the grill, go to the WiFi setting on your cell phone, and then connect with the grill by using your serial number as the password.
4. Go to the app of Electric Smoker, press the 'connect' button, and when connected, go to its setting and select the WiFi mode option and after few minutes, select the connect option again.
5. Prepare the grill, and for this, go to Electric Smoker app, set the temperature to 165 degrees F, and let it Heat.
6. When the grill has Heated, open its lid, place ribs on the grill by using a tong, shut with lid, and let it grill for 4 to 6 hours, turning halfway through.

7. Switch the temperature to 225 degrees F, continue grilling for 2 hours, then brush with chipotle sauce and continue grilling for 1 hour until glazed.
8. When done, let ribs rest for 30 minutes, then cut it into slices and serve.

Nutrition:
Calories: 668 Cal
Fat: 45 g
Carbs: 13 g
Protein: 48 g
Fiber: 0.3

58. Smoked Pork Chops in Lavender Balsamic Marinade

Preparation Time: 10 minutes
Cooking Time: 1 hour
Servings: 4
Ingredients:
- 2 tbsp. olive oil
- 3 tsp. cooking dry lavender
- 2 tsp. light brown sugar
- 2 tsp. fresh thyme, chopped
- Salt and grated black pepper
- 2 garlic cloves, finely chopped
- 4 pork chops or fillets
- 1/4 cup honey
- 2 tsp. balsamic vinegar

Directions:
1. In a bowl, combine oil, lavender, sugar, thyme, salt, pepper and garlic and mix well
2. Place the pork chops in a container then pour with the oil-lavender mixture.
3. Marinate at room temperature for one hour.
4. Meanwhile, in a pan, pour the honey and balsamic vinegar and cook over moderate to low heat until boiling. Set aside.
5. Take off the meat from marinade and pat dry with kitchen towel.
6. Smoke pork chops about 1 hour at 225°F.

7. Remove pork chops from grill and brush with honey balsamic mixture.
8. Roll the chops in aluminum foil and smoke the chops about 30 minutes, or until internal temperature reaches 145°F.
9. Let rest for 5 minutes and serve. Enjoy!

Nutrition:
Calories: 257.4
Fat: 31.4 g
Protein: 58.8 g
Carbs: 21.1 g

59. Smoked Pork Ribs with Hoisin Sauce

Preparation Time: 30 minutes
Cooking Time: 4 hours
Servings: 10
Ingredients:
- 5 lb. pork ribs
- 1/4 cup Hoisin sauce
- 3 tbsp. dry sherry
- 2 tbsp. soy sauce
- 2 tbsp. honey
- 1/4 cup water
- 2 garlic cloves, minced

Directions:
1. Cut the ribs into serving-size portions.
2. Place large plastic bag in a large bowl and combine Hoisin sauce, dry sherry, soy sauce, honey, water and minced garlic; stir.
3. Add the ribs, close bag tightly and shake several times.
4. Refrigerate 6 hours or overnight.
5. Drain ribs and reserve marinade.
6. Smoke for 3 hours at 225F, in Heated smoker.
7. After 3 hours, remove ribs, baste generously with reserved marinade and wrap in heavy-duty aluminum foil.

8. Return the meat to the smoker then cook for an additional 1 to 1 1/2 hours until internal temperature reaches 160F.
9. Serve hot. Enjoy!

Nutrition:
Calories: 553.9
Fat: 53.3 g
Protein: 35.5 g
Carbs: 7.1 g

60. Smoked Spiced Pork Tenderloin

Preparation Time: 15 minutes
Cooking Time: 2 hours 15 minutes
Servings: 6
Ingredients:

- 2 lb. pork tenderloin
- 1 tsp. garlic salt
- 1 tsp. onion powder
- 1 tsp. garlic powder
- 1 tsp. dry ginger
- Sea salt and fresh ground pepper

Directions:

1. Heat smoker to 225°F and add hickory wood chips.
2. Combine sea salt, black pepper, onion powder, dry ginger, garlic powder, and garlic salt to taste and season both sides of tenderloin.
3. Smoke unwrapped for 1 1/2 hours until internal temp reaches 150°F.
4. Remove from smoker and wrap with heavy-duty aluminum foil.
5. Place back into the smoker for an additional 30 minutes, or until internal temp reaches 165F.
6. When tenderloin is finished cooking, remove from the smoker, then let rest for 15 minutes.
7. Slice tenderloin into slices and serve hot. Enjoy!

Nutrition:
Calories: 307.9
Fat: 12.3 g
Protein: 45.3 g
Carbs: 0.9 g

61. BBQ Pulled Pork

Preparation Time: 20 minutes
Cooking Time: 15 hours
Servings: 7
Ingredients:

- 7 to 10 pounds pork butt, fat trimmed, at room temperature
- ½ cup apple cider vinegar
- Sea salt as needed
- Ground black pepper as needed
- ½ cup apple juice

For the Marinate:

- 2 tablespoons red pepper flakes
- 2 tablespoons onion powder
- 1 cup brown sugar
- 3 tablespoons paprika
- 5 tablespoons mustard paste
- 8 tablespoons olive oil

Directions:

1. Prepare the marinade, and for this, take a medium bowl, place all the ingredients in it and then whisk until well combined.
2. Rub the marinade on all sides of pork butt and then let it marinate for 12 to 24 hours in the refrigerator.
3. Then switch on the grill, go to the WiFi setting on your cell phone, and then connect with the grill by using your serial number as the password.
4. Go to the app of Electric Smoker, press the 'connect' button, and when connected, go to its setting and select the WiFi mode option and after few minutes, select the connect option again.

5. Prepare the grill, and for this, go to Electric Smoker app, set the temperature to 380 degrees F, and let it Heat.

6. Meanwhile, remove pork putt from the refrigerator, bring it to room temperature and then season it well with salt and black pepper.

7. When the grill has Heated, open its lid, place pork butt fat-side-up on the grill, shut with lid, and let it grill for 1 hour.

8. Meanwhile, pour apple juice in a small spray bottle, add apple cider vinegar, and then shake well.

9. Switch the temperature of the grill to 225 degrees F, spray with the apple juice mixture and then continue grilling for 5 hours or until the internal temperature reaches 160 degrees F.

10. Return pork butt from the grill, place it on a large piece of foil, spray with apple juice mixture, wrap it with foil and then continue grilling the pork until the internal temperature reaches 195 degrees F.

11. Once the app shows that the internal temperature of the chicken has reached 195 degrees F, open the grill and then transfer wrapped pork to a cutting board.

12. Let the pork rest for 30 minutes, uncover it, and then shred it by using two forks.

13. Serve straight away.

Nutrition:
Calories: 484 Cal
Fat: 21.6 g
Carbs: 46.2 g
Protein: 26.2 g
Fiber: 10.4 g

62. Pork Butt Honey Mustard Smoked Bites

Preparation Time: 30 minutes
Cooking Time: 5 hours
Servings: 6
Ingredients:

- Mustard, to taste
- 4 lb. Boston pork butt, no bones
- Butter, enough for the pork
- BBQ rub
- Brown sugar, to taste
- Honey, enough, for the pork
- BBQ sauce, to taste

Directions:

1. Prepare your Electric Smoker by Heating it to a temperature of about 250°F.

2. Carefully trim and remove excess fat from the pork.

3. Place the meat in a disposable aluminum pan and properly coat with BBQ rub and mustard.

4. Transfer the pan to your Heated smoker and give about 2–3 hours of smoking. Or you can aim to reach an internal temperature of about 160°F.

5. Take out the meat after smoking and cut small cubes and transfer to a fresh aluminum pan.

6. Include some of the cooking juice and some butter.

7. Spread BBQ sauce and honey, according to your taste. Coat with brown sugar.

8. Cover the pan with a thick aluminum foil and transfer to your smoker again.

9. Give another 80–90 minutes of smoking.

10. Take out and stir the meat bites and remove extra cooking juice.

11. Coat more sauce and transfer to your smoker again. You can increase the smoking temperature and reach up to 275°F.

12. Give about 25–32 minutes of smoking to get a caramelized texture.

13. Take out and allow to cool down for about 12–15 minutes.

14. Your dish is ready to be served. Enjoy!

Nutrition:
Calories: 257 Fat: 18 g
Protein: 15 g
Carbs: 8 g

63. Taquito Rolls with Creamy Pulled Pork

Preparation Time: 5 minutes
Cooking Time: 45 minutes
Servings: 6
Ingredients:

- 4 oz. cream cheese
- 1/2 lb. pulled pork
- 1/3 cup green salsa
- 1/2 cup cheddar cheese
- 1 pack small tortillas
- 1 lime

Directions:

1. Prepare your Electric Smoker by Heating it to a temperature of about 250°F.
2. Transfer the cream cheese to an over-friendly bowl and give about 30 seconds in the oven to get a soft texture.
3. In a large enough bowl, make a mixture of cheddar cheese, pulled pork, cream cheese, ½ lime juice, and salsa.
4. Use this mixture to make taquito rolls and seal each one of them tightly.
5. Put the rolls on a large aluminum sheet and transfer to your smoker.
6. Bake in the smoker for about 20–35 minutes. Make sure the edges start looking golden and crispy.
7. Take out and serve. Enjoy!

Nutrition:
Servings: 6
Total Time: 45 Minutes
Calories: 160
Fat: 7 g
Protein: 21 g
Carbs: 3 g

CHAPTER 6:

Beef Recipes

64.   Smoked Beef Ribs BBQ with Sweet Ginger Bourbon Tea
Preparation Time: 30 minutes
Cooking Time: 4 hours 30 minutes
Servings: 10
Ingredients:
- Beef Ribs (5-lb., 2.3-kg.)

The Rub
- Worcestershire sauce – 2 tablespoons
- Canola oil – 2 tablespoons
- Brown sugar – ¼ cup
- Sweet paprika – 2 tablespoons
- Black pepper – 1 tablespoon
- Kosher salt – 2 tablespoons
- Garlic powder – 2 teaspoons
- Onion powder – 2 teaspoons
- Cayenne powder – 1 teaspoon

The Glaze
- Ginger – 1 teaspoon
- Sweet tea – 1 cup
- Beef broth – ¾ cup
- Bourbon – ¾ cup
- Onion powder – 1 teaspoon
- Garlic powder – 1 teaspoon
- Diced parsley – 3 tablespoons
- Grated lemon zest – ½ teaspoon
- Lemon juice – 2 tablespoons

Directions:
1. Discard the excess fat from the beef ribs then baste Worcestershire sauce and canola oil over the beef ribs.
2. Combine the remaining rub ingredients—brown sugar, sweet paprika, black pepper, kosher salt, garlic powder, onion powder, and cayenne pepper then stir the mixture until well mixed.
3. Sprinkle the spice mixture over the beef ribs then set aside.
4. Next, plug in the Electric Smoker and press the power button to turn it on.
5. Press the "Temperature" button and set to 225°F (107°C).
6. After that, add wood chips to the smoker and pour water into the water pan.
7. Once the Electric Smoker is ready, place the seasoned beef ribs on the grill trays that are provided in the Electric Smoker then close the lid.
8. Smoke the seasoned beef ribs until the internal temperature has reached 130°F (54°C) for medium rare or 175°F (79°C) for well done. The smoking time will take approximately 4 hours and 30 minutes.
9. Check the wood chips level and add more wood chips if it is necessary.
10. In the meantime, place the entire glaze ingredients—ginger, sweet tea, bourbon, beef broth, onion powder, garlic powder, diced parsley, grated lemon zest, and lemon juice in a saucepan then bring to a simmer over low heat.
11. Stir the glaze mixture until incorporated and remove from heat.
12. After 6 hours of smoking, baste the glaze mixture over the beef ribs then continue smoking until the smoked beef reaches the desired internal temperature.
13. Once it is done, remove the smoked beef ribs from the Electric Smoker and transfer to a serving dish. Turn

the Electric Smoker off and allow it to cool.

14. Serve the smoked beef ribs and enjoy warm.

Nutrition:
Energy 607 kcal
Calcium, Ca37 mg
Magnesium, Mg36 mg
Phosphorus, P214 mg
Iron, Fe3.45 mg
Potassium, K477 mg
Sodium, Na1543 mg
Zinc, Zn6.19 mg

65. Super Spicy Smoked Brisket Garlic

Preparation Time: 30 minutes
Cooking Time: 4 hours 10 minutes
Servings: 10
Ingredients:
- Beef Brisket (4-lbs., 1.8-kg.)

The Marinade
- Chili powder – ¼ cup
- Cayenne pepper – 1 teaspoon
- Kosher salt – 1 ¼ tablespoons
- Brown sugar – 2 tablespoons
- Garlic powder – 2 tablespoons
- Cumin – 1 teaspoon
- Dried oregano – 1 tablespoon

Directions:
1. Combine the marinade ingredients—chili powder, cayenne pepper, kosher salt, brown sugar, garlic powder, cumin, and dried oregano in a bowl.
2. Rub the beef with the spice mixture then wrap tightly with plastic wrap.
3. Marinate the beef brisket overnight and store in the fridge to keep it fresh.
4. On the next day, take the marinated beef brisket out of the fridge then unwrap and thaw at room temperature.
5. Next, plug in the Electric Smoker and press the power button to turn it on.
6. Press the "Temperature" button and set to 225°F (107°C).

7. After that, add wood chips to the smoker and pour water into the water pan.
8. Place the seasoned beef brisket in the Electric Smoker and smoke until the internal temperature of the smoked beef brisket has reached 190°F (88°C).
9. The smoking time will take approximately 3 to 4 hours. Add more wood chips if it is needed.
10. Once it is done, remove the smoked beef brisket from the Electric Smoker and transfer to a serving dish.
11. Cut the smoked beef brisket into thick slices then serve.
12. Enjoy!

Nutrition:
Calcium, Ca30 mg
Magnesium, Mg33 mg
Phosphorus, P232 mg
Iron, Fe3.93 mg
Potassium, K634 mg
Sodium, Na3174 mg
Zinc, Zn5.39 mg

66. Juicy Crumbled Smoked Sirloin Beef Steak

Preparation Time: 10 minutes
Cooking Time: 5 hours
Servings: 10
Ingredients:
- Beef Sirloin (5-lb., 2.3-kg.)

The Marinade
- Balsamic vinegar – ½ cup
- Soy sauce – ½ cup
- Olive oil – ½ cup
- Worcestershire sauce – ¼ cup
- Honey – 2 tablespoons

- Italian seasoning – 2 teaspoons
- Garlic powder – 2 teaspoons
- Onion powder – 2 teaspoons
- Dried mustard – 2 teaspoons
- Brown sugar – 1 tablespoon
- Sweet paprika – 2 teaspoons
- Kosher salt – 1 ½ tablespoons

Directions:
1. Pour balsamic vinegar, soy sauce, olive oil, Worcestershire sauce, and honey into a zipper-lock plastic bag then season with Italian seasoning, garlic powder, onion powder, dried mustard, sweet paprika, and kosher salt. Stir the spice mixture until well combined.
2. Score the beef sirloin at several places then put it into the zipper-lock plastic bag.
3. Seal the zipper-lock plastic bag then shake until the beef sirloin is completely coated with the spice mixture.
4. Marinate the beef sirloin for at least 4 hours and store in the fridge to keep it fresh.
5. After 4 hours, remove the seasoned beef sirloin from the fridge and thaw at room temperature.
6. Next, plug in the Electric Smoker and press the power button to turn it on.
7. Press the "Temperature" button and set to 225°F (107°C).
8. After that, add wood chips to the smoker and pour water into the water pan.
9. Place the seasoned beef sirloin in the Electric Smoker and smoke for approximately 5 hours. Add more wood chips if it is necessary.
10. Once the smoked beef sirloin steak is tender or the internal temperature of the smoked beef sirloin steak has reached 190°F (88°C), take it out of the Electric Smoker.
11. Place the smoked beef sirloin steak on a serving dish and cut into thick slices.
12. Serve and enjoy immediately.

Nutrition:
Calcium, Ca74 mg
Magnesium, Mg59 mg
Phosphorus, P469 mg
Iron, Fe4.31 mg
Potassium, K864 mg
Sodium, Na1483 mg
Zinc, Zn8.24 mg

67. Savory Smoked Beef Chuck Roast With Red Wine Sauce

Preparation Time: 10 minutes
Cooking Time: 6 hours
Servings: 10
Ingredients:
- Beef Chuck Roast (4-lbs., 1.8-kg.)

The Rub
- Kosher salt – 1 ¼ tablespoons
- Pepper – 1 teaspoon

The Sauce
- Olive oil – 2 tablespoons
- Onion powder – 1 teaspoon
- Garlic powder – 1 ½ teaspoons
- Bay leaves -2
- Dried red wine – ½ cup
- Balsamic vinegar – 1 ½ teaspoons
- Worcestershire sauce – 2 teaspoons
- Soy sauce – 2 teaspoons
- Beef broth – ½ cup
- Brown sugar – a pinch

Directions:
1. Rub the beef chuck roast with salt and pepper then set aside.
2. Pour beef broth and olive oil into a heavy-duty aluminum pan then add onion powder, garlic powder, dried red wine, balsamic vinegar, Worcestershire sauce, soy sauce, and brown sugar. Stir the sauce until incorporated.
3. Next, plug in the Electric Smoker and press the power button to turn it on.
4. Press the "Temperature" button and set to 225°F (107°C).

5. After that, add wood chips to the smoker and pour beer into the water pan.

6. Place the seasoned beef chuck roast in the aluminum pan with sauce and flip until all sides of the beef chuck roast are completely coated with the sauce mixture.

7. Once the Electric Smoker is ready, place the aluminum pan with beef chuck roast in it and set the time to 6 hours. Smoke the beef chuck roast.

8. Regularly check the temperature of the Electric Smoker and add more wood chips if it is necessary.

9. Check the internal temperature of the smoked beef chuck roast and once it reaches 125°F (52°C), remove from the Electric Smoker.

10. Place the smoked beef chuck roast on a serving dish then drizzle the sauce on top.

11. Serve and enjoy warm.

Nutrition:
Calcium, Ca19 mg
Magnesium, Mg17 mg
Phosphorus, P137 mg
Iron, Fe1.87 mg
Potassium, K263 mg
Sodium, Na966 mg
Zinc, Zn5.99 mg

68. Butter Garlic Smoked Beef Rib Eye Rosemary
Preparation Time: 10 minutes
Cooking Time: 3 hours
Servings: 10
Ingredients:
- Beef Rib eye (5-lb., 2.3-kg.)

The Rub
- Minced garlic – 3 tablespoons
- Grated lemon zest – ½ teaspoon
- Dried thyme – 1 teaspoon
- Dried rosemary – 1 teaspoon
- Dried basil – 1 teaspoon
- Kosher salt – ¾ teaspoon
- Black pepper – ½ teaspoon

The Topping
- Cold butter cubes – 1 cup

Directions:
1. Rub the beef rib eye with minced garlic, grated lemon zest, dried thyme, dried rosemary, dried basil, kosher salt, and black pepper then place in a heavy-duty aluminum pan.
2. Sprinkle cold butter cubes over the seasoned beef rib eye and put fresh rosemary on top.
3. Plug in the Electric Smoker and press the power button to turn it on.
4. Press the "Temperature" button and set to 225°F (107°C).
5. After that, add wood chips to the smoker and pour water into the water pan. Add fresh rosemary to the water pan.
6. When the Electric Smoker is ready, place the aluminum pan in it then smoke the seasoned beef rib eye.
7. Set the time to 3 hours and once the internal temperature of the smoked beef rib eye has reached 125°F (52°C), remove it from the Electric Smoker.
8. Place the smoked beef rib eye on a serving dish then serve.
9. Enjoy warm.

Nutrition:
Calcium, Ca47 mg Magnesium, Mg43 mg
Phosphorus, P452 mg
Iron, Fe5.38 mg
Potassium, K769 mg
Sodium, Na505 mg
Zinc, Zn17.89 mg

69. Oak-Smoked Top Round
Preparation Time: 10 minutes
Cooking Time: 5 hours
Servings: 12
Ingredients:
- 12 hamburger buns
- 1 beef top round
- 3 Tbsp of melted butter
- Kosher salt, black pepper
- Horseradish sauce

Directions:

1. Add oak wood chips to the Wood Chips box, then plug the smoker and Heat it to 275°F.
2. Coat the meat with salt and pepper on the meat. Transfer the meat to the cooking grates and allow to smoke for about 5 hours. Or when the internal temperature of the beef records 145°F.
3. Transfer the meat to an aluminum foil. Let it rest for about 15-20 minutes. Brush the sides with melted butter.
4. Slice the meat thinly on the buns. Serve immediately

Nutrition:

Calories: 310 kcal Carbs: 32g
Fat: 50g
Protein: 46.5g.

70. Slam Dunk Brisket

Preparation Time: 20 minutes
Cooking Time: 9 hours
Servings: 8
Ingredients:

- 1/4 cup of Dijon mustard
- 7 pounds of brisket
- 1/4 cup of pickle juice
- 1 tsp of onion powder
- 1 tsp of garlic powder
- Barbecue sauce
- Kosher salt and black pepper

Directions:

1. Put the brisket on a chopping board and trim off the fat. Put the brisket on a baking sheet.
2. Get a bowl to mix the Dijon mustard and pickle juice. Rub the mixture on the brisket, then sprinkle salt and pepper.
3. Also, add onion powder and garlic powder to the brisket.
4. Heat the Electric Smoker to 275°F. Fill up the wood chip box. Transfer the brisket to the smoker to cook for about 8-9 hours until the internal temperature of the meat reads 165°F. Remove the brisket when it is ready.

5. Let it rest for about 1 hour. Slice the brisket in thick inches, then serve.

Nutrition:

Calories: 415kcal Fat: 41g
Carbs: 52.5g Protein: 38g

71. Smoked Beef Tenderloin

Preparation Time: 10 minutes
Cooking Time: 2 hours
Servings: 8
Ingredients:

- Cracked black pepper (ground)
- 2 Tbsp of olive oil
- 4 pounds of beef tenderloin
- Vegetable oil
- Kosher salt horseradish sauce

Directions:

1. Heat the Electric Smoker to 275°F.
2. Put the beef tenderloin on a baking sheet. Sprinkle with salt and pepper, then rub olive oil on all sides.
3. Transfer the beef tenderloin to the cooking grates of the smoker and allow it to smoke for about 2 hours. When the internal temperature of the meat records 180°F, remove them from the smoker and let it rest for 10 minutes.
4. Brush olive oil on the beef.
5. Put the beef on the serving place and serve accordingly.

Nutrition:

Calories: 390kcal Carbs: 50.5g
Protein: 43.5g Fat: 54g.

72. Texas style smoked beef brisket

Preparation Time: 30 minutes
Cooking Time: 18 hours
Servings: 20
Ingredients:

- 14 pounds whole brisket
- 2 tablespoons garlic powder

- 2 tablespoons ground black pepper
- 2 tablespoons kosher salt

Directions:
1. Remove fat or silver skin from brisket.
2. Combine garlic powder, pepper and salt.
3. Season beef with the mixture generously.
4. Heat smoker to 225 F.
5. Put beef on the smoker. Smoke for about 8 hours or until temperature reaches 165 F.
6. Remove beef from the smoker. Wrap in aluminum foil.
7. Put beef back on the smoker. Smoke for about 8 hours or until temperature reaches 200 F.
8. Remove beef from the smoker. Let it cool for 1 hour.
9. Slice meat and serve.

Nutrition:
Calories: 250
Total Fat: 19g
Saturated Fat: 7g
Protein: 18g
Carbs: 1g
Fiber: 0g
Sugar: 0g

73. Smoked Tri-Tip
Preparation Time: 20 minutes
Cooking Time: 2 hours
Servings: 6
Ingredients:
- 2 tsp of garlic powder
- 2 pounds of beef tri-tip
- 2 tsp of kosher salt
- 2 tsp of dried rosemary
- Olive oil
- Vegetable oil
- 1 tsp of dried oregano
- 2 tsp of ground pepper

Directions:
1. Heat the smoker to 275°F.
2. Mix the oregano, salt, garlic powder, pepper, and rosemary in a bowl. Brush the seasoning mix on the tri-tip.

3. Transfer the tri-tip to the Electric Smoker cooking grates. Smoke until the internal temperature is at 140°F for about 2 hours.
4. Remove the tri-tip from the smoker and place on aluminum foil. Let it rest for about 10 minutes.
5. Rub olive oil on all the sides of the tri-tip.
6. Serve it hot.

Nutrition:
Calories: 355 kcal
Carbs: 50g
Fat: 37.5g
Protein: 44g.

74. Smoked Bison Sirloin
Preparation Time: 10 minutes
Cooking Time: 4 hours
Servings: 8
Ingredients:
- 2 Tbsp of summer savory, thyme, rosemary, fresh herbs, and sage
- 6 pounds of bison sirloin
- 3 Tbsp of olive oil
- 3 Tbsp of spice rub
- Salt and black pepper

Directions:
1. Heat the smoker to a temperature of 275°F.
2. Brush the oil on the meat, then sprinkle with salt and pepper. Mix the other ingredients in a bowl, then rub the seasoning mix on the meat.
3. Transfer the meat to the cooking grates of the Electric Smoker; let it smoke for about 4 hours until the temperature of the beef records 160°F.
4. Remove it from the smoker. Cool for 20 minutes, then slice and serve.

Nutrition:
Calories: 325kcal
Carbs: 51.2g
Fat: 47g
Protein: 48g.

75.   Smoked Tenderloin Teriyaki

Preparation Time: 30 minutes
Cooking Time: 6 hours
Servings: 10
Ingredients:

- Beef tenderloin (4 ½ lbs., 2-kgs)

The Rub

- Brown sugar – 2 cups
- Worcestershire sauce – ½ cup
- Teriyaki sauce – 3 cups
- Liquid smoke flavoring – 1 teaspoon
- Meat tenderizer – ½ teaspoon

Directions:

1. Combine brown sugar with Worcestershire sauce, teriyaki sauce, liquid smoke flavoring, and meat tenderizer in a bowl. Mix well.
2. Rub the tenderloin with the spice then marinate overnight.
3. In the morning, remove the spiced tenderloin from the refrigerator then let it sit for about 30 minutes.
4. Heat an electric smoker to 225°F (107°C).
5. Wrap the spiced tenderloin with aluminum foil then place in the smoker.
6. Smoke the tenderloin for 6 hours and check once every hour. Add soaked hickory wood chips as needed.
7. After 6 hours and the internal temperature has reached 165°F (74°C), remove the smoked tenderloin from the smoker then place on a flat surface. Let it cool.
8. Once it is cool, cut the smoked tenderloin then arrange on a serving dish.
9. Serve and enjoy.

Nutrition:
Calcium, Ca108 mg
Magnesium, Mg104 mg
Phosphorus, P668 mg
Iron, Fe9.24 mg
Potassium, K1098 mg
Sodium, Na1815 mg
Zinc, Zn8.72 mg

76.   Cherry Smoked Strip Steak

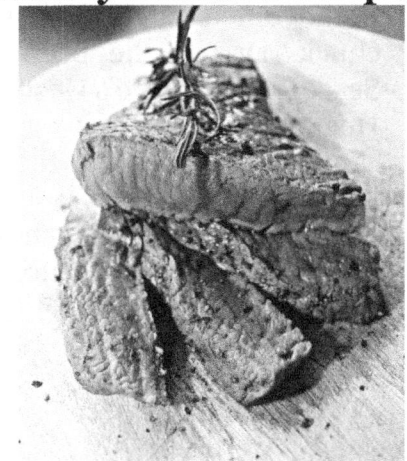

Preparation Time: 10 minutes
Cooking Time: 2 hours 30 minutes
Servings: 3
Ingredients:

- Kosher salt and black pepper
- 1 tsp of garlic powder
- 1 tsp of onion powder
- Olive oil
- 1-1/2 pound of boneless strip steak

Directions:

1. Add cherry wood chips to the Electric Smoker wood chip box, then Heat the smoker to 275°F.
2. Sprinkle salt and pepper on the steak. Add garlic powder and onion powder.
3. Place the steak in the smoker. Let it smoke for about 90 minutes until an internal temperature of 180°F is measured.
4. Remove the steak from the smoker and rub it with olive oil. Let it rest for about 15 minutes.
5. Serve immediately.

Nutrition:
Calories: 402kcal Fat: 44.5g
Carbs:5 9g Protein: 49g.

77.   Meaty Chuck Short Ribs

Preparation Time: 20 minutes
Cooking Time: 5 hours
Servings: 4
Ingredients:

- 4 Tbsp of olive oil
- 4 pounds of beef chuck short rib
- 4 Tbsp of Pete's western rub

Directions:

1. Remove excess fat on the beef chuck. Drizzle the beef with oil. Season it with Pete's western rub.
2. Heat the Electric Smoker to 275°F. Transfer the rib to the smoker racks.
3. Let it smoke for about 5 hours until the internal temperature reaches 180°F.
4. Let the rib rest for about 20 minutes before serving.

Nutrition:
Calories: 287kcal
Carbs: 40g
Protein: 37g
Fat: 31g.

78. Barbecue Smoked Beef Chuck

Preparation Time: 10 minutes
Cooking Time: 5 hours
Servings: 10
Ingredients:

- 5 pounds beef chuck roll
- 1/3 cup ground black peppercorn
- ¼ cup kosher salt

Directions:

1. Combine pepper and salt.
2. Season beef with the mixture generously.
3. Heat smoker to 275 F.
4. Put beef on the smoker. Smoke for about 4 hours or until temperature reaches 165 F.
5. Remove beef from the smoker. Wrap in aluminum foil.
6. Put beef back on the smoker. Smoke for about 5 hours or until temperature reaches 140 F.
7. Remove beef from the smoker. Let it cool for 30 minutes.
8. Slice meat thinly.
9. Serve with onion, pickles and white bread.

Nutrition:
Calories: 422 Total Fat: 24g
Saturated Fat: 10g Protein: 47g
Carbs: 0g Fiber: 0g
Sugar: 0g

79. Smoked Pete-zza Meatloaf

Preparation Time: 10 minutes
Cooking Time: 8 hours
Servings: 8
Ingredients:

- 1 cup of pizza sauce
- 1 pound of ground beef
- 1/2 tsp of salt
- 1/2 tsp of garlic powder
- 1 cup of bread crumb
- 2 big eggs
- 1/2 tsp of ground pepper
- 2 Tbsp of olive oil
- 3 ounces of pepperoni sausage
- 2 cups of mozzarella cheese
- 1 cup of portobello mushroom
- 2 cups of shredded cheddar
- 2/3 cup of green bell pepper
- 1/2 cup of red bell pepper
- 2/3 cup of red onion, sliced

Directions:

1. In a medium bowl, add the eggs, ground pepper, 1/2 cup of pizza sauce, garlic powder, and salt. Whisk together.
2. Get a skillet, heat the olive oil, fry the red bell pepper, mushroom, green bell pepper, and red onion for about 2 minutes. Sprinkle salt and black pepper on the mixture.
3. Get a parchment paper, put the meatloaf on it, then top with pepperoni, place the fried vegetables, and mozzarella. Roll the meatloaf with the parchment paper.
4. Heat the smoker to 275°F. Place the wrapped meatloaf on the smoker rack. Smoke it for about 1 hour. Check if the internal temperature is at 180°F.
5. Remove the meatloaf. Let it rest for about 10 minutes. Serve it with 1/2 cup of pizza sauce.

Nutrition:
Calories: 345kcal
Carbs: 31g
Protein: 48g
Fat: 36g.

80. Smoked Prime Rib
Preparation Time: 15 minutes
Cooking Time: 3 hours
Servings: 6
Ingredients:
- Ground black pepper
- Kosher salt
- Onion powder and garlic powder
- 6 pounds of prime rib
- 2 Tbsp of olive oil
- Horseradish sauce
- Smoked jus

Directions:
1. Rub the ribs with salt and black pepper, add garlic powder and onion powder, then brush with olive oil.
2. Heat the Electric Smoker to 275°F. Transfer the seasoned rib to the cooking racks.
3. Smoke the rib for 3 hours 15 minutes until it records an internal temperature of 135°F
4. Remove the rib from the smoker. Place it on the serving dish and trim off excess fat lumps. Serve.

Nutrition:
Calories: 291kcal
Fat: 24g
Protein: 20g
Carbs: 30g.

81. Smoked Corned Beef
Preparation Time: 30 minutes
Cooking Time: 4 hours
Servings: 10
Ingredients:
- Beef brisket (5 lbs., 2.3-kgs)

The Brine
- Cold water – 2 ½ quarts
- Beer – 3 bottles
- Chopped onion – ½ cup
- Salt – 1 ¼ cups
- Brown sugar – ¾ cup
- Pickling spice – ¼ cup
- Minced garlic – 2 ½ tablespoons

The Braising
- Beer – ¾ bottle
- Chopped onion – ¼ cup
- Brown sugar – 2 ½ tablespoons
- Pickling spice – 1 ½ tablespoons
- Minced garlic – 2 tablespoons
- Black pepper – 1 teaspoon

Directions:
1. Place chopped onion, salt, brown sugar, pickling spice and minced garlic in a bowl.
2. Pour beer and cold water over the spices then mix until incorporated.
3. Soak the beef brisket in the spice liquid then marinate overnight.
4. In the morning, Heat an electric smoker to 250°F(120°C).
5. Place the soaked beef brisket then place on the smoker's rack.
6. Smoke the beef brisket for 2 ½ hours. Add more soaked wood chips if it is necessary.
7. Meanwhile, combine the entire braising ingredients then pour into a disposable aluminum foil.
8. After the beef brisket has been smoked for 2 ½ years. Take the beef out of the smoker then place in the braising mixture.
9. Return the beef brisket to the smoker and smoke for an hour and a half.
10. Once it is done and the internal temperature is 145°F (60°C), remove the smoked beef from the smoker then place on a flat surface. Let it cool for a few minutes.
11. When the beef brisket is already cool, cut the smoked corned beef into thin slices then arrange on a serving platter.
12. Serve and enjoy.

Nutrition:
Calcium, Ca52 mg
Magnesium, Mg12 mg
Phosphorus, P28 mg
Iron, Fe0.44 mg
Potassium, K114 mg
Sodium, Na14350 mg
Zinc, Zn0.14 mg
Copper, Cu0.05 mg

82.   Smoked Beef Stew
Preparation Time: 30 minutes
Cooking Time: 10 hours
Servings: 8
Ingredients:
- 2 pounds stewing beef, cubed
- 5 cups beef broth
- 1 can diced tomatoes
- 8 carrots, peeled and diced
- 8 medium potatoes, peeled and diced
- 2 onions, diced
- 2 tablespoons corn starch
- 2 tablespoons water

For the rub:
- 1 tablespoon paprika
- 1 tablespoon sugar
- 2 teaspoon dry oregano
- 1 teaspoon garlic powder
- 1 teaspoon ground black pepper
- 1 teaspoon salt
- ½ teaspoon cayenne pepper
- ½ teaspoon thyme

Directions:
1. Combine rub ingredients.   Mix thoroughly.
2. Season beef with the mixture generously.
3. Heat smoker to 225 F.
4. Put beef on the smoker. Smoke for about 2 hours.
5. Remove beef from the smoker. Put in a slow cooker.
6. Add beef broth, tomatoes, carrots, potatoes and onions.
7. Cook for 8 hours on low heat.
8. Whip corn starch and water together. Add to the slow cooker 15 minutes before finishing the stew.
9. Serve with fresh bread.

Nutrition:
Calories: 386
Total Fat: 18g
Saturated Fat: 6g
Protein: 52g
Carbs: 28g
Fiber: 4g
Sugar: 2g

83.   Smoked Beef Jerky

Preparation Time: 10 minutes
Cooking Time: 7 hours
Servings: 6
Ingredients:
- 2 pounds sirloin, sliced ½ inch thick
- 1 cup soy sauce
- 4 tablespoons ground black pepper
- 1 tablespoon cider vinegar
- 1 dash hot pepper sauce
- 1 dash Worcestershire sauce

Directions:
1. Combine all ingredients in except for the beef. Mix well.
2. Add beef slices. Cover and place in the fridge overnight.
3. Heat smoker to 170 F.
4. Put beef on the smoker. Smoke for about 7 hours or until jerky edges appear dry.

Nutrition:
Calories: 220 Total Fat: 4g
Saturated Fat: 2g Protein: 28g
Carbs: 6g Fiber: 0g Sugar: 3g

84.   Smoked Meatloaf Tomato
Preparation Time: 10 minutes
Cooking Time: 2 hours
Servings: 10
Ingredients:
- Ground beef (2 ½ lbs., 1.3-kgs)

The Spice
- Diced tomato – ½ cup
- Organic eggs – 2
- Chopped onion – ¼ cup
- Breadcrumbs – ¼ cup
- Salt – 3 teaspoons
- Black pepper – 2 teaspoons
- Paprika – 1 teaspoon

The Sauce
- Tomato puree – ¼ cup
- Diced tomato – 2 tablespoons
- Sugar – 1 ½ tablespoons
- Pepper – ½ teaspoon
- Nutmeg – ½ teaspoon
- Chopped onion – ¼ cup

Directions:
1. Heat an electric smoker to 225°F (110°C) and coat a medium loaf pan with cooking spray.
2. Place ground beef in a food processor then add diced tomato, eggs, chopped onion, and breadcrumbs.
3. Season with salt, black pepper, and paprika then pulse to combine.
4. Transfer the mixture to the prepared loaf pan then spread evenly.
5. Place the loaf pan in the smoker then smoke for 2 hours.
6. Meanwhile, place all of the sauce ingredients in a saucepan then stir well. Bring to a simmer then set aside.
7. Monitor the internal temperature and when it reaches 160°F (70°C), remove the meatloaf from the smoker.
8. Let the meatloaf cool then transfer to a serving dish.
9. Drizzle the sauce over the meatloaf then enjoy.

Nutrition:
Calcium, Ca43 mg Magnesium, Mg30 mg Phosphorus, P245 mg Iron, Fe3.82 mg Potassium, K437 mg Sodium, Na799 mg Zinc, Zn7.36 mg

85. Smoked Beef Bites With Brown Sauce
Preparation Time: 12 hours
Cooking Time: 1 hour 10 minutes
Servings: 10
Ingredients:
- Beef Steak (5 lbs., 2.3-kgs)

The Marinade
- Red wine vinegar – 3 cups
- Olive oil – 1 cup

The Sauce
- Butter – 3 ½ tablespoons
- Sliced shallots – 2 teaspoons
- Dry red wine – 1 ½ cups
- Beef broth – 1 ½ cups
- Thyme – ½ teaspoon
- Flour – 2 tablespoons
- Black pepper – 1 teaspoon
- Salt – ¼ teaspoon

Directions:
1. Cut the beef steak into medium cubes then place in a container with a lid.
2. Combine red wine vinegar with olive oil then pour the mixture over the beef cubes.
3. Marinade the beef cubes for 12 hours. Store in a refrigerator to keep them fresh.
4. Heat an electric smoker to 250°F (121°C).
5. After 12 hours, take the beef out from the refrigerator.
6. Transfer the beef cubes to a disposable aluminum pan and discard the marinade.
7. When the smoker has reached the desired temperature, place the pan in the smoker and smoke the beef cubes for an hour.
8. Meanwhile, cook the sauce.
9. Heat a saucepan over medium heat then add butter to the saucepan.
10. Once the butter is melted, stir in sliced shallot then sauté until wilted and aromatic.
11. Pour beef broth and dry red wine over the shallot then season with salt, black pepper, and thyme. Bring to boil.
12. Once it is boiled, take about ½ cup of the gravy then add flour into it. Mix well.
13. Pour the flour mixture into the saucepan and stir to combine. Remove from heat.
14. When the smoked beef is done, remove from the smoker then transfer to a serving dish.

15. Serve with the brown sauce then enjoy.

Nutrition:
Calcium, Ca16 mg
Magnesium, Mg12 mg
Phosphorus, P69 mg
Iron, Fe1.6 mg
Potassium, K174 mg
Sodium, Na151 mg
Zinc, Zn1.46 mg

86. Sweet Smoked Roast Black Pepper

Preparation Time: 30 minutes
Cooking Time: 5 hours
Servings: 10
Ingredients:
- Round beef roast (5 lbs., 2.3-kgs)

The Rub
- Salt – 2 ½ teaspoons
- Black pepper – 2 tablespoons
- Sugar – 1 tablespoon
- Onion powder – 1 ½ tablespoons
- Cayenne pepper – 1 ½ teaspoons

The Gravy
- Beef broth – 1 cup
- Chopped onion – ½ cup
- Apple juice – 1 cup
- Olive oil – 3 tablespoons

Directions:
1. Heat an electric smoker to 230°F (110°C).
2. Combine the rub ingredients then rub the beef roast.
3. Wrap the seasoned beef roast with aluminum foil then place on the smoker's rack.
4. Smoke the beef roast for 5 hours or until the internal temperature has reached 165°F (74°C).
5. Take the beef roast out from the smoker then let it warm for a few minutes.
6. Meanwhile, sprinkle chopped onion in a disposable aluminum pan then pour beef broth, apple juice, and olive oil over the chopped onion.

7. Unwrap the beef roast and place in the disposable aluminum pan.
8. Return the beef roast back to the smoker then smoke for 5 hours.
9. Once it is cooked, remove from the smoker then let it cool
10. Cut the smoked beef roast into slices then serve.
11. Enjoy.

Nutrition:
Calcium, Ca18 mg
Magnesium, Mg7 mg
Phosphorus, P13 mg
Iron, Fe1.12 mg
Potassium, K91 mg
Sodium, Na640 mg
Zinc, Zn0.09 mg

87. Smoked Beef Ribs

Preparation Time: 30 minutes
Cooking Time: 5 hours 30 minutes
Servings: 3
Ingredients:
- Beef ribs (10 lbs., 4.5-kgs)
- The Rub
- Red wine vinegar – 3 cups
- Olive oil – 1 cup
- The Sauce
- Salt – 1 tablespoon
- Brown sugar – ½ cup
- Garlic powder – 1 ½ tablespoons
  Onion powder – 1 ½ tablespoons
- Black pepper – 1 ¼ tablespoons
- Onion powder – 1 ½ tablespoons

Directions:
1. Heat the electric smoker to 225°F (107°C).
2. Combine salt with brown sugar, onion powder, garlic powder, and black pepper then rub the beef ribs with the mixture. Let it sit for about 30 minutes.
3. Place the seasoned ribs on a smoker's rack then smoke for 4 hours.
4. After 4 hours, take the beef ribs from the smoker then carefully wrap with aluminum foil.
5. Return then beef ribs to the smoker then smoke again for about an hour

and a half or until the internal temperature has reached 160°F (71°C).

6. Remove the smoked beef ribs from the smoker then let it warm for a few minutes.
7. Unwrap the smoked beef ribs then transfer to a serving dish.
8. Serve and enjoy.

Nutrition:
Calcium, Ca37 mg
Magnesium, Mg35 mg
Phosphorus, P213 mg
Iron, Fe3.32 mg
Potassium, K425 mg
Sodium, Na794 mg
Zinc, Zn6.15 mg

88.   Smoked Roast Beef

Preparation Time: 20 minutes
Cooking Time: 5 hours
Servings: 8
Ingredients:
- 3 pounds beef rump roast
- For the rub:
- 1 ½ teaspoon salt
- 1 teaspoon garlic powder
- 1 teaspoon pepper
- 1 teaspoon smoked paprika
- ½ teaspoon onion powder
- Worcestershire sauce

Directions:
1. Combine all ingredients except for the Worcestershire sauce. Mix well.
2. Rub beef with Worcestershire sauce. Season with the mixture.
3. Heat smoker to 200 F.

4. Put beef on the smoker. Smoke for about 5 hours or until temperature reaches 150 F.
5. Remove beef from the smoker. Let it cool for 20 minutes.
6. Slice and serve.

Nutrition:
Calories: 298
Total Fat: 10g
Saturated Fat: 4g
Protein: 46g
Carbs: 19g
Fiber: 0g
Sugar: 10g

89.   Smoked Beef Burnt Ends
Preparation Time: 15 minutes
Cooking Time: 10 hours
Servings: 6
Ingredients:
- 3 pounds chuck roast
- ½ cup barbecue sauce
- ¼ cup brown sugar
- 2 tablespoons brown sugar

For the rub:
- 1 tablespoon garlic powder
- 1 tablespoon ground black pepper
- 1 tablespoon kosher salt

Directions:
1. Heat smoker to 275 F.
2. Combine rub ingredients.
3. Season beef generously with the rub mixture.
4. Put beef on the smoker. Smoke for about 5 hours or until temperature reaches 165 F.
5. Remove beef from the smoker. Wrap in aluminum foil.
6. Put beef back on the smoker. Smoke for about 1 hour or until temperature reaches 195 F.
7. Remove beef from the smoker. Let it cool for 20 minutes.
8. Slice and transfer to a foil pan.
9. Sprinkle with ¼ cup sugar and drizzle with barbecue sauce.
10. Put pan on the smoker, close lid and cook for 2 hours.

11. Sprinkle with 2 tablespoons sugar and drizzle with barbecue sauce.
12. Stir and grill for a few minutes.

Nutrition:
Calories: 208 Total Fat: 5g
Saturated Fat: 2g Protein: 30g
Carbs: 11g Fiber: 0g Sugar: 11g

90. Grass-Fed Beef Sirloin Kebabs

Preparation Time: 25 minutes
Cooking Time: 3 minutes
Servings: 4
Ingredients:

- 1 pound grass-fed top sirloin steak, trimmed
- 8 skewers
- Cooking spray
- 2 tablespoons olive oil
- 1 teaspoon ground coriander
- 1 teaspoon black pepper
- ¾ teaspoon kosher salt

For the sauce:

- ½ cup plain 2% reduced-fat Greek yogurt
- 2 tablespoons fresh dill, chopped
- 1 tablespoon fresh lemon juice
- 1 tablespoon lemon rind, grated
- ¼ teaspoon kosher salt

Directions:

1. Heat smoker to 550 F.
2. Combine sauce ingredients. Mix thoroughly.
3. Cut steak into 16 strips. Mix with oil, coriander, pepper and salt.
4. Thread 2 steak strips into each skewer.
5. Put skewers on the smoker coated with cooking spray. Smoke for about 90 seconds on each side.
6. Serve with yogurt sauce.

Nutrition:
Calories: 244 Total Fat: 14g
Saturated Fat: 6g
Protein: 27g
Carbs: 4g
Fiber: 0g
Sugar: 3g

91. Smoky Caramelized Onion Burgers

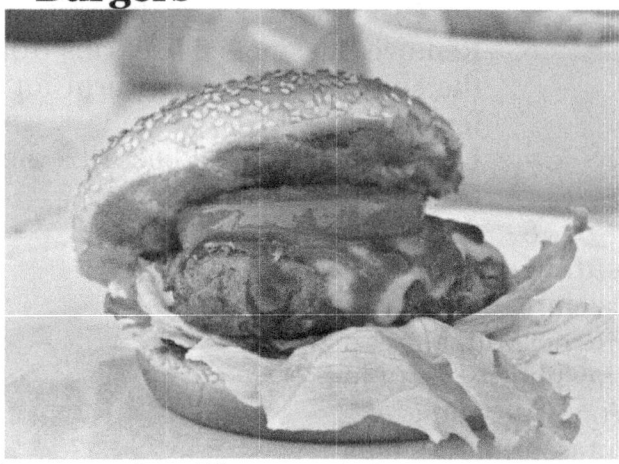

Preparation Time: 25 minutes
Cooking Time: 20 minutes
Servings: 4
Ingredients:
For the patties:

- 1 pound 90% lean ground sirloin
- 1 ½ cups yellow onion, thinly sliced
- 1 ½ tablespoons minced garlic
- ½ tablespoon ground cumin
- ½ tablespoon olive oil
- 1 teaspoon smoked paprika
- 1 teaspoon kosher salt
- 1 teaspoon ground black pepper
- Cooking spray

For the burgers:

- 4 whole-wheat hamburger buns
- 4 tomato slices
- 2 red onion slices
- 1 cup baby arugula leaves
- 2 tablespoons canola mayonnaise
- 2 tablespoons roasted red bell pepper, finely chopped
- 1 tablespoon minced fresh chives

Directions:

1. Heat smoker to 450 F.
2. In a skillet, put oil over medium heat. Sauté yellow onion until golden brown.
3. Add garlic, cook until fragrant.
4. Remove skillet from heat. Let cool. Put onion mixture in a large bowl.
5. Add the rest of patty ingredients. Mix thoroughly.
6. Shape beef mixture into 4 patties.

7. Coat smoker with cooking spray. Put patties on the smoker. Smoke for 4 minutes on each side.
8. Remove patties from the smoker.
9. In a bowl, mix bell pepper, mayonnaise and chives. Mix thoroughly.
10. Put patties on bottom halves of buns. Layer with tomato, red onion, arugula, mayonnaise mixture and top halves of buns.

Nutrition:
Calories: 340
Total Fat: 26g
Saturated Fat: 10g
Protein: 23g
Carbs: 29g
Fiber: 1g
Sugar: 5g

92. Smoked Pulled Beef
Preparation Time: 10 minutes
Cooking Time: 12 hours
Servings: 10
Ingredients:
- 6 pounds chuck roast
- 3 cups beef stock
- 1 yellow onion, sliced

For the rub:
- 2 tablespoons black pepper
- 2 tablespoons garlic powder
- 2 tablespoons kosher salt

Directions:
1. Heat smoker to 225 F.
2. Combine the rub ingredients. Mix thoroughly.
3. Season beef roast generously with the rub mixture.
4. Put beef on the smoker. Smoke for about 3 hours.
5. Spray with 1 cup of beef stock every hour while smoking.
6. Spread sliced onions in an aluminum pan. Pour 2 cups of beef stock. Place the beef roast on top of the onions.
7. Put the pan on the smoker. Increase temperature to 250 F.
8. Smoke for about 3 hours or until temperature reaches 165 F.
9. Cover the pan tightly with aluminum foil. Continue smoking for 5 hours or until temperature reaches 202 F.

Nutrition:
Calories: 422
Total Fat: 24g
Saturated Fat: 10g
Protein: 47g
Carbs: 0g
Fiber: 0g
Sugar: 0g

CHAPTER 7:

Fish and Seafood Recipes

93. Brined Bass
Preparation Time: 9 hours
Cooking Time: 4 hours
Servings: 6
Ingredients:
- 2 pounds striped bass fillets, gutted and scaled
- 1/3 cup salt
- 1/4 cup brown sugar
- 1 tablespoon ground black pepper
- 2 dried bay leaves
- 2 slices of lemon
- 4 cups filtered water
- 1/2 cup dry white wine

Directions:
1. Place a pot at high heat, pour in water, add salt and sugar and bring the mixture to a low boil or until salt and sugar are dissolved completely.
2. Then remove the pot from heat, cool brine at room temperature and transfer into a large container with a lid.
3. Add lemon slices along with black pepper, bay leaves and wine, stir until mixed, then add bass, pour in more water to cover fillets completely and let soak for 4 to 8 hours in the refrigerator, covering the container.
4. Then remove the bass from brine, rinse well, pat dry with paper towels and let rest for 45 minutes at room temperature.
5. In the meantime, plug in the smoker, fill its tray with hickory wood chips and water pan halfway through, and place dripping pan above the water pan.
6. Then open the top vent, shut with lid and use temperature settings to Heat smoker at 180 degrees F.
7. Place bass fillets on smoker rack, insert a meat thermometer, then shut with lid and set the timer to smoke for 2 to 4 hours or until meat thermometer registers an internal temperature between 145 to 160 degrees F.
8. Check vent of smoker every hour and add more wood chips and water to maintain temperature and smoke.
9. Serve straightaway.

Nutrition:
Calories: 25 Cal
Carbs: 0 g
Fat: 2 g
Protein: 4 g
Fiber: 0 g.

94. Cured Salmon
Preparation Time: 14 hours
Cooking Time: 6 minutes
Servings: 3
Ingredients:
- 1 ½ pound salmon filet, skinless and boneless
- 1 bunch of fresh dill, chopped
- 1/2 of lemon, thinly sliced
- 1/4 cup salt
- 1/4 cup brown sugar
- 2 tablespoons ground black pepper

Directions:
1. Stir together salt, black pepper, and sugar and rub this mixture all over the salmon filet.
2. Place seasoned salmon into a shallow baking dish, top with lemon slices and with dill, and wrap

top with plastic wrap and then the whole dish.

3. Place this dish into the refrigerator to marinate salmon for 8 to 12 hours.

4. Then remove the dish from the refrigerator, uncover it, rinse fillet well, pat dry and let rest at room temperature for 2 hours.

5. When ready to cook, plug in the smoker, fill its tray with pecan wood chips and water pan halfway through, and place dripping pan above the water pan.

6. Then open the top vent, shut with lid and use temperature settings to Heat smoker at 160 degrees F.

7. Place salmon on smoker rack, insert a meat thermometer, then shut with lid and set the timer to smoke for 3 to 6 hours or until meat thermometer register an internal temperature of 130 degrees F.

8. Check vent of smoker every hour and add more wood chips and water to maintain temperature and smoke.

9. Serve straightaway.

Nutrition:
Calories: 210 Cal Carbs: 0 g
Fat: 12.3 g Protein: 22.5 g Fiber: 0 g

95. Shrimps

Preparation Time: 15 minutes
Cooking Time: 30 minutes
Servings: 6
Ingredients:

- 2 pounds shrimp, peeled, deveined and rinsed
- 2 tablespoons lemon juice
- 2 tablespoons chopped parsley
- 2 tablespoons onion powder
- 2 tablespoons garlic powder
- ¼ cup sea salt
- 3 tablespoons paprika
- 3 tablespoons ground black pepper
- 2 teaspoons cayenne pepper
- 2 tablespoons dried thyme
- 2 tablespoons olive oil

Directions:

1. Take a large foil pan, grease with oil and then place shrimps in it.

2. Stir together remaining ingredients except for lemon juice and sprinkle this mixture on all over shrimps until evenly coated.

3. Then Plug in the smoker, fill its tray with hickory wood chips and water pan halfway through, and place dripping pan above the water pan.

4. Then open the top vent, shut with lid and use temperature settings to Heat smoker at 250 degrees F.

5. Drizzle 1 tablespoon lemon juice over shrimps, then place the pan on smoker rack, then shut with lid and set the timer to smoke for 30 minutes or until shrimps are opaque, stirring halfway through.

6. When done, remove the pan from the smoker, drizzle remaining lemon juice over shrimps and serve.

Nutrition:
Calories: 60 Cal Carbs: 0 g
Fat: 2 g,
Protein: 10 g
Fiber: 0 g.

96. Smoked Red Fish Fillets

Preparation Time: 16 hours
Cooking Time: 1 hour
Servings: 2
Ingredients:

- 2 fillets of redfish with skin, each about 12 ounces
- 1 teaspoon garlic powder
- 1/2 cup salt
- 1 teaspoon ground black pepper
- 1/2 cup brown sugar

- 1 teaspoon dried lemon zest
- 1 lemon, sliced

Directions:

1. Stir together garlic powder, salt, black pepper, sugar, and lemon zest until combined.
2. Take a glass baking dish, spread 1/3 of prepared spice mixture in the bottom, then later with one fillet, skin-side down and press lightly.
3. Sprinkle half of remaining spice mixture over the fillet in pan, then top with another filet, flesh-side down and then sprinkle remaining spice mixture on top of it and around the side of fish.
4. Close the dish with plastic wrap and then let marinate in the refrigerator for 8 to 12 hours.
5. Remove marinated fish from the dish, rinse well, and pat dry using paper towels.
6. Return fish into the refrigerator for 2 to 3 hours or until dried and then bring fish to room temperature for 45 minutes.
7. When ready to cook, plug in the smoker, fill its tray with hickory wood chips and water pan halfway through, and place dripping pan above the water pan.
8. Then open the top vent, shut with lid and use temperature settings to Heat smoker at 120 degrees F.
9. Place fish on smoker rack, insert a meat thermometer, then shut with lid and set the timer to smoke for 1 hour or more until meat thermometer registers an internal temperature of 140 degrees F.
10. Check vent of smoker every hour and add more wood chips and water to maintain temperature and smoke.
11. Serve straightaway.

Nutrition:
Calories: 27 Cal Carbs: 0 g
Fat: 0.5 g Protein: 5.3 g
Fiber: 0 g.

97. Lemon Pepper Tuna

Preparation Time: 1 hour
Cooking Time: 4 hours 10 minutes
Servings: 6
Ingredients:

- 6 tuna steaks, each about 6 ounces
- 3 tablespoons salt
- 3 tablespoons brown sugar
- 1/4 cup olive oil
- ¼ cup lemon pepper seasoning
- 1 teaspoon minced garlic
- 12 slices of lemon

Directions:

1. Season tuna with salt and sugar until evenly coated on all sides, then place in a dish and cover with plastic wrap.
2. Place dish into the refrigerator for 4 hours or overnight, then rinse well and pat dry and coat well with garlic powder, lemon pepper seasoning, and oil.
3. Plug in the smoker, fill its tray with peach wood chips and water pan halfway through, and place dripping pan above the water pan.
4. Then open the top vent, shut with lid and use temperature settings to Heat smoker at 120 degrees F.
5. In the meantime,
6. Place seasoned tuna on smoker rack, insert a meat thermometer, then shut with lid and set the timer to smoke for 1 hour or more until meat thermometer registers an internal temperature of 140 degrees F.
7. Check vent of smoker every hour and add more wood chips and water to maintain temperature and smoke.
8. When done, transfer tuna to a cutting board, let rest for 10 minutes and then serve with lemon slices.

Nutrition:
Calories: 275 Cal Carbs: 0.6g
Fat: 23 g
Protein: 17 g
Fiber: 0 g.

98. Seasoned Shrimp Skewers

Preparation Time: 10 minutes
Cooking Time: 35 minutes
Servings: 4
Ingredients:

- 1 ½ pound fresh large shrimp, peeled, deveined and rinsed
- 2 tablespoons minced basil
- 2 teaspoons minced garlic
- 1/2 teaspoon sea salt
- 1/2 teaspoon ground black pepper
- 1/3 cup olive oil
- 2 tablespoons lemon juice

Directions:

1. Place basil, garlic, salt, black pepper and oil in a large bowl, whisk until well combined, then add shrimps and toss until well coated.
2. Fill the smoker tray with hickory wood chips and water pan with water and white wine halfway through, and place dripping pan above the water pan.
3. Then open the top vent, shut with lid and use temperature settings to Heat smoker at 225 degrees F.
4. Thread shrimps on wooden skewers, six shrimps on each skewer.
5. Place shrimp skewers on smoker rack, then shut with lid and set the timer to smoke for 35 minutes or shrimps are opaque.
6. When done, drizzle lemon juice over shrimps and serve.

Nutrition:
Calories: 168 Cal Carbs: 2 g
Fat: 11 g Protein: 14 g Fiber: 0 g.

99. Marinated Trout

Preparation Time: 7 hours

Cooking Time: 3 hours
Servings: 8
Ingredients:

- 4 pounds trout fillets
- 1/2 cup salt
- 1/2 cup brown sugar
- 2 quarts water

Directions:

1. Pour water in a large container with lid, add salt and sugar and stir until salt and sugar are dissolved completely.
2. Add trout, pour in more water to submerge trout in brine and refrigerate for 4 to 8 hours, covering the container.
3. Then remove trout from brine, rinse well and pat dry with paper towels.
4. Place trout on a cooling rack, skin side down, and cool in the refrigerator for 2 hours or until dried.
5. Then remove trout from the refrigerator and bring to room temperature.
6. In the meantime, plug in the smoker, fill its tray with maple wood chips and water pan halfway through, and place dripping pan above the water pan.
7. Then open the top vent, shut with lid and use temperature settings to Heat smoker at 160 degrees F.
8. In the meantime, place trout on smoker rack, insert a meat thermometer, then shut with lid and set the timer to smoke for 2 ½ to 3 hours or more until meat thermometer registers an internal temperature of 145 degrees F.
9. Check vent of smoker every hour and add more wood chips and water to maintain temperature and smoke.
10. Serve straightaway.

Nutrition:
Calories: 49 Cal Carbs: 0 g Fat: 1.2 g
Protein: 8.8 g Fiber: 0 g.

100. Smoked Salmon Recipe

Preparation Time: 15 minutes
Cooking Time: 4 hours
Servings: 5
Ingredients:

- 1 to 1 ½ - pound whole salmon filet, skin and bones removed
- 1 - shot (jigger) unflavored vodka or tequila
- ¼ - cup kosher salt
- ¼ - cup brown or raw turbinado sugar
- 2 - tsp cracked black pepper
- 1 - bunch of fresh dill, chopped
- ½ - lemon, thinly sliced
- Alder wood chips

Directions:

1. Spot the entire salmon filet in a shallow preparing dish, ideally glass or earthenware. Pour the liquor over the filet.
2. Blend salt, pepper, and sugar together and pat everywhere throughout the salmon. Top with the lemon cuts. Spot the dill in addition and tenderly press down.
3. Spread the highest point of the salmon firmly with cling wrap, tucking it down into the dish. Spot another layer of the fold around the dish to seal it firmly.
4. Spot the salmon in the icebox medium-term for roughly 8 to 12 hours.

Nutrition:
Calories: 223
Carbs: 4g
Fat: 19g
Protein: 9g

101. Smoked Cajun Spiced Shrimp

Preparation Time: 10 minutes
Cooking Time: 30 minutes
Servings: 6
Ingredients:

- 2 - lbs large or jumbo cleaned shrimp
- ¼ - cup sea salt
- 3 - tsp paprika
- 3 - tsp cracked black pepper
- 2 - tsp garlic powder
- 2 - tsp onion powder
- 2 - tsp dried thyme
- 2 - tsp cayenne pepper (adjust to your liking)
- Butter
- 1 - lemon of Juice
- Chopped fresh parsley

Directions:

1. Whenever solidified, defrost the shrimp. Strip and devein the shrimp if no longer effectively arranged. Pat the shrimp dry.
2. Join the dry fixings in a field with a top. Shake until every one of the fixings is mixed properly.
3. Coat the foil field, or skillet, with both margarine and olive oil. Spot the shrimp inside the box. Spoon as a splendid a part of the dry rub over the shrimp, as required, to coat it. Any extra dry rub will shop exceptional at the off danger which you don't make use of everything. Hurl the shrimp to coat the 2 aspects. Set the box apart at the same time as you set up the smoker.
4. Set up the smoker by using adding timber chips to the plate and water to the bowl. Heat the smoker to somewhere inside the range of 225°F and 250°F. Open the top vent.
5. While the smoker is up to temperature, press 1/2 of the lemon squeeze over the shrimp and Set the dish in the smoker. Cook for 15mins. Give the shrimp a mix. Cook for a further 15mins until the shrimp is misty crimson.
6. Take the dish and crush the rest of the lemon squeeze at the shrimp. Include the parsley and serve a platter with cornmeal and a plate of combined vegetables.
7. Two or three first-rate side dishes for Cajun-spiced shrimp are gooey cornmeal and a harsh veggies plate of blended veggies. You could make

these at the same time as the shrimp is smoking. Teach the shrimp a lesson over the cornmeal.

Nutrition:
Calories: 133
Carbs: 0g
Fat: 6g
Protein: 18g

102. Smoked Greek-Style Shrimp

Preparation Time: 10 minutes
Cooking Time: 30 minutes
Servings: 6
Ingredients:

- 2 - lbs large shrimp, cleaned
- 3 - tsp good extra virgin olive oil
- 3 - TBS butter, melted
- ½ - fresh lemon o Juice
- 5 - garlic cloves, minced
- 1 - TBS dried oregano
- 1/3 - cup flat-leaf parsley, chopped
- 1 - tsp sea or coarse kosher salt
- 1 ½ - cups crumbled feta cheese
- EVOO for serving
- Fresh lemon wedges for serving

Directions:

1. Set up the smoker by adding wood chips to the plate and water to the bowl. Heat the smoker to somewhere in the range of 225°F and 250°F. Open the top vent.
2. Whenever solidified, defrost the shrimp. Strip and devein the shrimp if not officially arranged. Pat the shrimp dry.
3. In an enormous bowl, combine the EVOO, spread, and lemon juice. Permit cooling. Blend in the garlic, oregano, parsley, and salt. Add the shrimp and hurl to coat equitably. Spot the shrimp in the container or dish with the majority of the sauce.
4. At the point when the smoker is up to temperature, place the dish in the smoker. Cook for 15 minutes. Give the shrimp a mix. Include the feta cheddar top and smoke for an additional 15 minutes until the

shrimp is an obscure pink and the cheddar is somewhat dissolved.

5. Take the dish out from the smoker and spot the shrimp and all the skillet squeezes on a serving platter or bowl. Shower with EVOO and present with lemon wedges and side dishes.

Nutrition:
Calories: 379
Carbs: 43g
Fat: 9g
Protein: 32g

103. Smoked Ahi Tuna Steaks

Preparation Time: 4 hours
Cooking Time: 2 hours 15 minutes
Servings: 5
Ingredients:

- 6 - Ahi tuna steaks, approximately 1 - inch thick and weighing approximately 4 to 6 - ounces each
- 3 - TBS kosher salt
- 3 - TBS light brown sugar or raw turbinado sugar
- ¼ - cup extra virgin olive oil (EVOO)
- Lemon pepper seasoning in a shaker jar
- 1 - tsp ground garlic
- 12 - thin slices of fresh lemon

Directions:

1. Coat the fish steaks with the salt and sugar on all sides. Spot these in a fixed holder or baggie and refrigerate for 4 hours or medium-term.
2. Add water to the skillet in your smoker. Spot wood contributes to the plate. Heat the smoker to 190°F.
3. Take the fish steaks to a clean surface and wipe up a huge portion of the dry saline solution. Coat the two sides with EVOO, lemon pepper flavoring, and garlic powder.
4. Set the fish steaks legitimately on the smoker rack and put 2 cuts of lemon over every steak. Spot the

rack back in the smoker. Smoke for 60 minutes.

5. At 60 minutes, check the interior temperature with a computerized thermometer. You are searching for 140 to 145°F. Keep on smoking until you accomplish that temperature. This will take roughly from 60 to 105 minutes.

6. Take to a slicing board to rest for only a couple of minutes. Present with new lemon wedges, corn salsa, and cuts of ready avocado.

Nutrition:
Calories: 140
Carbs: 0g
Fat: 2g
Protein: 29g

104. Smoked Seasoned Shrimp Skewers

Preparation Time: 15 minutes
Cooking Time: 35 minutes
Servings: 4
Ingredients:
- 1 ½ - lbs large shrimp, approximately 25 to 30 count fresh or frozen (thawed)
- 1/3 - cup good extra virgin olive oil (EVOO)
- 4 - garlic cloves, minced
- 2 - TBS minced fresh basil leaves
- ½ - tsp sea salt
- ½ - tsp cracked black pepper
- Dry white wine for smoking
- Lemon for serving

Directions:
1. Spot the EVOO, garlic, basil, salt, and pepper in a big bowl. Whisk collectively.
2. Clean the shrimp by using evacuating the shells and eliminating the intestinal tract from the again of the shrimp.
3. Add the shrimp to the bowl and hurl to coat with the dressing. Put in a safe spot at the same time as you drench your sticks and installation your smoker.

4. Take a rack out from the smoker to place the sticks on. Set up your smoker through including timber chips to the plate and half of water + half white wine to the bowl.
5. Heat the smoker to 225°F. Open the pinnacle vent.
6. Set up to six shrimp on every stick via penetrating the top stop and the final component. They need to resemble the letter C mendacity degree.
7. Spot the shrimp sticks on the rack and placed the rack inside the smoker. Smoke for 35 minutes, or till the shrimp are surely murky and a crimson/white tone.
8. Crush some lemon over the shrimp before serving.

Nutrition:
Calories: 260
Carbs: 2g
Fat: 17g
Protein: 25g

105. Brined & Smoked Trout Fillets

Preparation Time: 7 hours
Cooking Time: 3 hours
Servings: 8
Ingredients:
- 4 - pounds of river, approximately 8 filets
- 2 - quarts filtered water
- ½ - cup of kosher salt
- ½ - cup brown sugar

Directions:
1. Take the stick bones from the trout fillets.
2. Consolidate the salt, sugar, and water in a huge compartment, kind of 1 to 2-gallon length. Blend nicely until the salt and sugar have disintegrated. Submerge the trout fillets in the saline solution and unfold the holder. Refrigerate for three and as long as 8hrs.
3. Take the trout from the salt water and wash below virus water. Expel the overabundance dampness from

the filets with smooth paper towels. Spot the trout filets, skin aspect down, on a cooling rack this is fitted inside a sheet dish. Spot the skillet inside the fridge for 2 hours and as much as medium-term.

4. Take 2 racks from the smoker and see the filets at the racks pores and skin facet down. Enable the fish to relaxation while you set up the smoker. Fill the water bowl half manner. Spot wood contributes to the plate. Birch, maple, or very well feature admirably. Open the pinnacle vent. Turn the smoker on and Heat to one 160°F.

5. Set the racks with fish within the smoker. Cook the trout for 2 1/2 to 3hrs or until the fish arrives at an inner temperature of one hundred 45°F. Renew the wood chips and water as required, probable like clockwork.

6. Serve the smoked fish with toasted loaf cuts and an invigorating, inexperienced plate of blended vegetables. You can acquire canapé crostini by means of placing a bit serving of blended veggies at the toasts and setting a few cuts of fish on the pinnacle.

Nutrition:
Calories: 150 Carbs: 0g
Fat: 6g
Protein: 22g

106. Tender Salmon Fillet

Preparation Time: 10 minutes
Cooking Time: 60 minutes
Servings: 4

Ingredients:
- 1 ½ lbs salmon fillet
- 1 tsp black pepper
- 1 tbsp Dijon mustard
- 1 tsp kosher salt

Directions:
1. Heat the smoker to 225 F/ 107 C using the cherry wood chips.
2. Season salmon with mustard, pepper, and salt.
3. Place salmon in the smoker and cook until internal temperature reaches to 145 F.
4. Serve and enjoy

Nutrition:
Calories: 229
Total Fat: 10.7g
Saturated Fat: 1.5g
Protein: 33.2g
Carbs: 0.6g
Fiber: 0.3g
Sugar: 0g

107. Flavorful Smoked Trout

Preparation Time: 15 minutes
Cooking Time: 2 hours
Servings: 4
Ingredients:
- 1 lb trout
- 1 tsp black pepper
- 1 tsp fennel seeds
- 1 tsp mustard seeds
- 1 tbsp olive oil
- 1 tsp kosher salt

Directions:
1. Heat the smoker to 225 F/ 107 C using the applewood chips.
2. Coarsely grind the spices.
3. Brush fish with oil and rub with ground spices.
4. Place fish into the smoker and cook for 11/2 to 2 hours or until internal temperature reaches to 125 F.
5. Serve and enjoy.

Nutrition:
Calories: 252 Total Fat: 13.4g
Protein: 30.6g
Carbs: 0.9g
Saturated Fat: 2.2g
Fiber: 0.5g
Sugar: 0.1g

108. Garlic Herb Shrimp

Preparation Time: 10 minutes
Cooking Time: 30 minutes
Servings: 4
Ingredients:

- 1 lb fresh shrimp, peeled and deveined
- 1 tsp garlic powder
- 1 tbsp dried basil
- 1 tbsp dried oregano
- 2 tbsp olive oil
- 1 tsp salt

Directions:

1. In a bowl, toss shrimp with oil, garlic powder, basil, oregano, and salt.
2. Transfer shrimp in foil pan.
3. Heat the smoker to 225 F/ 107 C using the alder wood chips.
4. Place shrimp into the smoker and cook for 30 minutes.
5. Serve and enjoy

Nutrition:
Calories: 201 Total Fat: 9.1g
Saturated Fat: 1.6g Protein: 26.1g
Carbs: 3g Fiber: 0.6g Sugar: 0.2g

109. Smoked Scallops

Preparation Time: 10 minutes
Cooking Time: 20 minutes
Servings: 6
Ingredients:

- 2 lbs scallops
- Pepper
- Salt

Directions:

1. Heat the smoker to 225 F/ 107 C using the cherry wood chips.
2. Season scallops using the pepper and salt and place into the smoker and cook for 20 minutes.
3. Serve and enjoy.

Nutrition:
Calories: 133
Total Fat: 1.2g Saturated Fat: 0.1g
Protein: 25.4g
Carbs: 3.6g
Fiber: 0g
Sugar: 0g

110. Garlic Prawns

Preparation Time: 10 minutes
Cooking Time: 30 minutes
Servings: 4
Ingredients:

- 24 large prawns
- 4 garlic cloves, minced

For rub:

- 1 tsp onion powder
- 1 tsp garlic powder
- 2 tsp paprika
- ¼ cup brown sugar
- 1 tbsp kosher salt

Directions

1. Mix together all rub ingredients.
2. Add garlic and prawns into the bowl and toss well to coat. Place in the refrigerator for 1-2 hours.
3. Heat the smoker to 200 F/ 93 C using the hickory wood chips.
4. Thread marinated prawns onto the soaked wooden skewers then place into the smoker.
5. Cook for 30 minutes and serve.

Nutrition:
Calories: 86 Total Fat: 0.7g
Saturated Fat: 0.2g
Protein: 8.1g
Carbs: 12g
Fiber: 0.6g
Sugar: 9.3g

111. Crab Legs

Preparation Time: 10 minutes
Cooking Time: 30 minutes
Servings: 4
Ingredients:

- 6 lbs crab legs

- 2 tbsp sweet rub
- 2 lemon juice
- 6 garlic cloves, minced
- ¼ cup fresh basil, chopped
- 1 cup butter, melted

Directions:
1. Heat the smoker to 225 F/ 107 C using the cherry wood chips.
2. Place crab legs in a foil pan.
3. Mix together butter, basil, garlic, lemon juice, and sweet rub and pour over crab legs.
4. Place in smoker and cook for 30 minutes.
5. Serve and enjoy

Nutrition:
Calories: 596 Total Fat: 11g
Saturated Fat: 28g Protein: 32g
Carbs: 11g Fiber: 2g Sugar: 1g

112. Healthy & Delicious Smoke Salmon

Preparation Time: 10 minutes
Cooking Time: 2 hours
Servings: 6
Ingredients:
- 1 salmon fillet
- 1 tsp chili powder
- 1 tbsp garlic powder
- ¼ cup sugar
- ½ cup brown sugar
- ½ tsp paprika
- 2 tbsp salt

Directions:
1. Mix together chili powder, garlic powder, sugar, brown sugar, paprika, and salt.
2. Rub chili powder mixture over the salmon fillet.
3. Heat the smoker to 225 F/ 107 C using the cherry wood chips.
4. Place salmon in the smoker and cook for 2 hours.
5. Serve and enjoy

Nutrition:
Calories: 123 Total Fat: 1.9g
Saturated Fat: 0.3g Protein: 6.1g
Carbs: 21.5g Fiber: 0.4g
Sugar: 20.4g

113. Herb Marinade Fish Fillets

Preparation Time: 10 minutes
Cooking Time: 2 hours 30 minutes
Servings: 4
Ingredients:
- 4 catfish fillets

For marinade:
- 3 tbsp sugar
- 1 tsp cayenne pepper
- 1 tsp black pepper
- 1 tbsp basil
- 1 tbsp thyme
- 2 tbsp oregano
- 2 garlic cloves, minced
- 1 lemon juice
- ½ cup red wine vinegar
- 1 cup olive oil
- 1 tbsp salt

Directions:
1. Mix together all marinade ingredients.
2. Place fish fillets in marinade and coat well. Place in the refrigerator for 1 hour. Heat the smoker to 225F using the alder wood chips.
3. Place marinated fish fillets in the smoker and cook for 2 hours 30 minutes. Serve and enjoy.

Nutrition:
Calories: 702 Total Fat: 62.9g
Saturated Fat: 9.5g Protein: 25.4g
Carbs: 12.3g Fiber: 1.5g; Sugar: 9.3g

114. Smoked Whole Snapper With Chimichurri Recipe

Preparation Time: 15 mins
Cooking Time: 3 hours
Servings: 4
Ingredients:
- 4 to 5- lb. whole snapper, scaled and gutted

- 2 - TBS butter at room temperature
- 2 - TBS extra virgin olive oil (EVOO)
- ½ - fennel bulb + fronds, woody stalks and core discarded, sliced thinly
- ½ - small white or yellow onion, sliced thinly
- 1 - Whole lemon sliced thinly into rounds
- 1 ½ - tsp sea salt
- 1 - tsp cracked black pepper

Directions:
1. In a medium container, integrate the margarine and EVOO. Include the salt and pepper. Cut the fennel, onion, and lemon. Save a portion of the verdant fennel fronds.
2. Set up your smoker by means of adding timber chips to the plate and water to the bowl. Heat the smoker to 225F. Open the pinnacle vent.
3. Liberally coat within and outside of the fish with the margarine and EVOO + salt and pepper. Stuff the hole with the fennel cuts, onion, fennel fronds, and 1/2 of the lemon cuts. Spot the fish on 2 sheets of aluminum foil. Turn up the rims of the foil to maintain the dampness in.
4. Set the fish at the foil pontoon within the smoker on the center rack. Cook for three to 4 hours until the internal temperature arrives at 145 to a hundred and 50F. This is roughly 45 minutes for every pound of fish.
5. Serve the fish complete or spot it on a reducing board and filet it, taking the backbone and any stick bones. And serve it on a platter with chimichurri sauce and pureed potatoes

Nutrition:
Calories: 127
Carbs: 0g
Fat: 3g
Protein: 25g

115. Smoked Tilapia
Preparation Time: 10 minutes
Cooking Time: 2 hours
Servings: 4
Ingredients:
- 4 tilapia fillets
- 1 cup brown sugar
- 2 tbsp fish sauce
- ¼ cup olive oil
- 3 garlic cloves
- 1 tbsp ginger root, peeled and chopped
- 2 grapefruits, peeled and quartered
- ½ tsp salt

Directions:
1. Add grapefruit, brown sugar, fish sauce, garlic, ginger, and salt into the blender and blend until smooth.
2. In a large bowl, place tilapia fillets. Pour blended mixture over tilapia fillets and coat well. Put in the refrigerator for 2 hours.
3. Heat the smoker to 275 F135 C using the alder wood chips.
4. Place tilapia fillets in the smoker and cook for 2 hours.
5. Serve and enjoy.

Nutrition:
Calories: 414
Total Fat: 14.7g
Saturated Fat: 2.8g
Protein: 33.1g
Carbs: 42g
Fiber: 0.8g
Sugar: 40g

116. Teriyaki Fish Fillets
Preparation Time: 10 minutes
Cooking Time: 2 hours
Servings: 4
Ingredients:
- 4 tilapia fillets
- 1 tbsp sriracha sauce
- 2/3 cup honey
- 1 cup teriyaki sauce

Directions:

1. In a shallow dish, mix together teriyaki sauce, sriracha, and honey until well blended.
2. Add fish fillets in the dish and coat well with marinade. Place in the refrigerator for 2 hours.
3. Heat the smoker to 275 F/ 135 C using the alder wood chips.
4. Place marinated fish fillets in the smoker and cook for 2 hours.

Nutrition:
Calories: 401
Total Fat: 4.5g
Saturated Fat: 1.4g
Protein: 36.4g
Carbs: 58g
Fiber: 0.2g;
Sugar: 56.8g

117. Flavorful Smoked Tilapia

Preparation Time: 10 minutes
Cooking Time: 2 hours
Servings: 6
Ingredients:

- 6 tilapia fillets
- ½ tsp lemon pepper
- ½ tsp garlic powder
- 2 tbsp fresh lemon juice
- 3 tbsp olive oil
- 1 tsp kosher salt

Directions:

1. Heat the smoker to 225F/ 107C using the maple wood chips.
2. Mix together oil, lemon pepper, garlic powder, lemon juice, and salt.
3. Brush oil mixture onto both sides of the fish fillets.
4. Place fish fillets in the smoker and cook for 1 ½ to 2 hours.
5. Serve and enjoy.

Nutrition:
Calories: 202
Total Fat: 9.1g
Saturated Fat: 2g
Protein: 32.1g
Carbs: 0.4g
Fiber: 0.1g
Sugar: 32.1g

118. Tasty Buttery Shrimp

Preparation Time: 10 minutes
Cooking Time: 25 minutes
Servings: 4
Ingredients:

- 15 large shrimp
- 2 tbsp fresh lemon juice
- 1 tbsp Italian seasoning
- 2 rosemary spring
- 2 garlic cloves, minced
- ½ cup butter, melted

Directions:

1. Heat the smoker to 275 F/ 135 C using the pecan wood chips.
2. Add all ingredients into the large bowl and toss well.
3. Transfer shrimp mixture into the foil pan. Place in smoker and cook for 20-25 minutes.
4. Serve and enjoy.

Nutrition:
Calories: 243
Total Fat: 24.5g
Saturated Fat: 14.9g
Protein: 5.1g
Carbs: 1.4g
Fiber: 0.1g
Sugar: 0.5g

119. Chipotle Shrimp

Preparation Time: 10 minutes
Cooking Time: 30 minutes
Servings: 4
Ingredients:

- 1 ½ lbs jumbo shrimp, peeled and deveined
- 4 tbsp butter, melted
- 2 tbsp fresh lime juice
- 2 tbsp olive oil
- 2 tsp chipotle chili, chopped
- 2 garlic cloves, minced
- 2 green onion, minced
- 3 tbsp fresh parsley, chopped
- Pepper
- Salt

Directions:

1. Heat the smoker to 250 F/ 135 C using pecan wood chips.

2. Add all ingredients into the large bowl and toss well. Transfer shrimp mixture into the foil pan and place into the smoker.
3. Cook shrimp for 30 minutes.
4. Serve and enjoy

Nutrition:
Calories: 289
Total Fat: 18.6g
Saturated Fat: 8.3g
Protein: 30.8g
Carbs: 1.3g
Fiber: 0.3g
Sugar: 3.3g

120. Smoked Halibut
Preparation Time: 10 minutes
Cooking Time: 45 minutes
Servings: 6
Ingredients:
- 4 lbs fresh halibut fillets
- ½ cup white wine
- 2 garlic cloves, minced
- 6 tbsp butter, melted
- Pepper
- Salt

Directions:
1. In a shallow dish, mix together butter, garlic, pepper, and salt.
2. Place fish fillets in the dish and coat well. Place in the refrigerator for 1 hour.
3. Heat the smoker to 225 F/ 107 C using alder wood chips.
4. Place marinated fish fillets in the smoker and cook for 45 minutes or until internal temperature reaches to 140 F.
5. Serve and enjoy.

Nutrition:
Calories: 219
Total Fat: 13.3g
Saturated Fat: 7.3g
Protein: 20.9g
Carbs: 0.9g
Fiber: 0g
Sugar: 0.2g

121. Smoked Tuna

Preparation Time: 10 minutes
Cooking Time: 7 hours
Servings: 4
Ingredients:
- 4 tuna steaks
- 1-gallon water
- 1 cup honey
- ¼ tsp garlic, chopped
- 1 1/8 cup sugar
- 1 tsp pepper
- 3/8 cup salt

Directions:
1. Add all ingredients except tuna steaks into the pot and stir well.
2. Add tuna steaks. Cover and place in the refrigerator for overnight.
3. Heat the smoker to 140 F/ 60 C using the applewood chips.
4. Place marinated tuna steaks in the smoker and cook for 7 hours.
5. Serve and enjoy.

Nutrition:
Calories: 700
Total Fat: 19.3g
Saturated Fat: 4.5g
Protein: 8.1g
Carbs: 133.2g
Fiber: 0.9g
Sugar: 125.9g

122. Smoked Snapper Fillet
Preparation Time: 10 minutes
Cooking Time: 60 minutes
Servings: 6
Ingredients:
- 1 ½ lbs red snapper fillets
- 1 tbsp garlic, granulated
- 3 tbsp brown sugar

- 2 quarts water
- 1 tbsp maple syrup
- 1 tbsp black pepper
- 2 tbsp olive oil
- Kosher salt

Directions:

1. For the brine: Add water, salt, garlic, and 2 tbsp brown sugar in a pot and stir well.
2. Add fish fillets in brine and set aside for 2 hours.
3. Mix together olive oil, 1 tbsp brown sugar, and pepper and rub over fish fillets.
4. Heat the smoker to 225 F/ 107 C using the applewood chips.
5. Place fish fillets in the smoker and cook for 60 minutes.
6. Brush fish fillets with maple syrup and serve.

Nutrition:
Calories: 216
Total Fat: 6.7g
Saturated Fat: 1.1g
Protein: 30g
Carbs: 7.8g
Fiber: 0.3g
Sugar: 6.4g

123. Delicious Trout Fillets

Preparation Time: 10 minutes
Cooking Time: 3 hours
Servings: 4
Ingredients:

- 4 trout fillets
- 1 tsp lemon pepper
- ¼ cup teriyaki sauce
- ¼ cup soy sauce
- 2 cups of water
- ½ tbsp salt

Directions:

1. In a bowl, mix together water, soy sauce, teriyaki sauce, and salt.
2. Place fish fillets in a bowl. Cover and place in the refrigerator. Store for overnight.
3. Heat the smoker to 225 F/ 107 C using the alder wood chips.
4. Place marinated fish fillets in the smoker and cook for 3 hours.
5. Serve and enjoy.

Nutrition:
Calories: 144
Total Fat: 5.3g
Saturated Fat: 0.9g
Protein: 18.6g
Carbs: 4.4g
Fiber: 0.3g
Sugar: 2.8g

CHAPTER 8:

Vegetables And Sides

124. Smashed Potato Casserole
Preparation Time: 30 minutes
Cooking Time: 45 – 60 minutes
Servings: 8
Ingredients:

- 1 small red onion, thinly sliced
- 1 small green bell pepper, thinly sliced
- 1 small red bell pepper, thinly sliced
- ¾ cup sour cream
- 1 small yellow bell pepper, thinly sliced
- 3 cups mashed potatoes
- 8 - 10 bacon
- ¼ cup bacon grease or salted butter (½ stick)
- 1 ½ teaspoons barbecue rub
- 3 cups shredded sharp cheddar cheese (divided)
- 4 cups hash brown potatoes (frozen)

Directions:

1. Get that bacon cooking over medium heat in a large skillet. Cook till nice and crisp. Aim for 5 minutes on both sides. Then set aside your bacon. Put the bacon grease into a glass container and set aside.
2. Using the same skillet, warm up the butter or bacon grease over medium heat. When warm enough, sauté bell peppers and red onions. You're aiming for al dente. When done, set it all aside.
3. Grab a casserole dish, preferably one that is 9 by 11 inches. Spray with some nonstick cooking spray, then spread the mashed potatoes out, covering the entire bottom of the dish.
4. Add the sour cream to the next layer over the potatoes. When you're done, season it with some of the barbecue rub.
5. Create a new layer with the sautéed veggies over the potatoes.
6. Sprinkle your sharp cheddar cheese—just 1½ of the cups. Then add the frozen hash brown potatoes.
7. Scoop out the rest of the bacon grease or butter from the sautéed veggies, all over the hash browns, and then top it all off with some delicious crumbled bacon bits. Set up your electric smoker for indirect cooking. Heat to 350°F.
8. Add the remaining of the sharp cheddar cheese (1½ cups) over the whole thing, and then use some aluminum foil to cover the casserole dish.
9. Set up your smoker for indirect cooking. Heat to 350°F.
10. Let the whole thing bake for 45 - 60 minutes. Ideally, you want the cheese to bubble.
11. Move it out and let it sit for about 10 minutes.

Nutrition:
Calories: 232
Fat: 2g
Carbs: 48g
Protein: 9g
Intolerances:
Gluten-Free, Egg-Free

125. Buffalo Mini Sausages

Preparation Time: 30 minutes
Cooking Time: 1 hour 30 minutes
Servings: 10
Ingredients:

- 8 ounces regular cream cheese (room temp)
- ¾ cup cheddar cheese blend and shredded Monterey Jack (not necessary)
- 1 teaspoon smoked paprika
- 1 teaspoon garlic powder
- ½ teaspoon red pepper flakes (not necessary)
- ¾ cup sour cream
- Little Smokies sausages (20)
- 10 bacon strips, thinly sliced and halved
- 10 jalapeno peppers (medium)

Directions:

1. Wash the jalapenos, then slice them up along the length. Get a spoon, or a paring knife if you prefer, and use that to take out the seeds and the veins.
2. Place the scooped-out jalapenos on a veggie grilling tray and put it all aside.
3. Get a small bowl and mix the shredded cheese, cream cheese, paprika, cayenne pepper, garlic powder, and red pepper flakes. Mix them thoroughly.
4. Get your jalapenos which you've hollowed out, and then stuff them with the cream cheese mix.
5. Get your little Smokies sausage, and then put it right onto each of the cheese stuffed jalapenos.
6. Grab some of the thinly sliced and halved bacon strips and wrap them around each of the stuffed jalapenos and their sausage.
7. Grab some toothpicks. Use them to keep the bacon nicely secured to the sausage.
8. Set up your smoker so it's ready for indirect cooking. Get it Heated to 250°F.
9. Put your jalapeno peppers in and smoke them at 250°F for anywhere from 90 minutes to 120 minutes. You want to keep it going until the bacon is nice and crispy.
10. Take out the atomic buffalo turds, and then let them rest for about 5 minutes.
11. Serve!

Nutrition:
Calories: 198
Fat: 17g
Cholesterol: 48mg
Carbs: 3g
Protein: 8g
Intolerances:
Egg-Free

126. Brisket Baked Beans
Preparation Time: 20 minutes
Cooking Time: 1 hour 30 minutes
Servings: 10
Ingredients:

- 1 green bell pepper (medium, diced)
- 1 red bell pepper (medium, diced)
- 1 yellow onion (large, diced)
- 2 - 6 jalapeno peppers (diced)
- 1 can baked
- 2 tablespoons olive oil (extra-virgin)
- 3 cups brisket flat (chopped)
- beans (28 ounces)
- 1 can red kidney beans (1 40ounces, rinsed, drained)
- 1 cup barbecue sauce
- ½ cup brown sugar (packed)
- 2 teaspoons mustard (ground)
- 3 cloves of garlic (chopped)
- 1 ½ teaspoon black pepper
- 1 ½ teaspoon kosher salt

Directions:

1. Put a skillet on the fire, on medium heat. Warm up your olive oil. Toss in the diced jalapenos, peppers, and onions. Stir every now and then for 8 minutes.
2. Grab a 4-quart casserole dish. Now, in your dish, mix in the pork and beans, kidney beans, baked beans, chopped brisket, cooked peppers

and onions, brown sugar, barbecue sauce, garlic, mustard, salt, and black pepper.
3. Heat your smoker to 325°F.
4. Cook your brisket beans, for 90 minutes to 120 minutes. Keep it uncovered as you cook. When it's ready, you'll know, because the beans will get thicker and will have bubbles as well.
5. Rest the food for 15 minutes, before you finally move on to step number 6.
6. Serve!

Nutrition:
Calories: 200
Fat: 2g
Cholesterol: 10mg
Carbs: 35g
Protein: 9g

127. Twice-Baked Spaghetti Squash

Preparation Time: 15 minutes
Cooking Time: 45 minutes
Servings: 2
Ingredients:
- 1 spaghetti squash (medium)
- 1 tablespoon olive oil (extra virgin)
- 1 teaspoon salt
- ½ teaspoon pepper
- ½ cup Parmesan cheese (grated, divided)
- ½ cup mozzarella cheese (shredded, divided)

Directions:
1. Cut the squash along the length in half. Make sure you're using a knife that's large enough, and sharp enough. Once you're done, take out the pulp and the seeds from each half with a spoon.
2. Season the insides of each half of the squash with some olive oil.

When you're done with that, sprinkle the salt and pepper.
3. Heat your smoker to 375°F.
4. Put each half of the squash on the grill. Make sure they're both facing upwards on the grill grates, which should be nice and hot.
5. Bake for 45 minutes, keeping it on the grill until the internal temperature of the squash hits 170°F. You'll know you're done when you find it easy to pierce the squash with a fork.
6. Move the squash to your cutting board. Rest for 10 minutes, so it can cool a bit.
7. Turn up the temp on your smoker to 425°F.
8. Using a fork to remove the flesh from the squash in strands by raking it back and forth. Do be careful, because you want the shells to remain intact. The strands you rake off should look like spaghetti, if you're doing it right.
9. Put the spaghetti squash strands in a large bowl, and then add in half of your mozzarella and half of your Parmesan cheeses. Combine them by stirring.
10. Take the mix, and stuff it into the squash shells. When you're done, sprinkle them with the rest of the Parmesan and mozzarella cheeses.
11. Optional: You can top these with some bacon bits, if you like.
12. Allow the stuffed spaghetti squash shells you've now stuffed to bake at 435°F for 15 minutes.
13. Serve and enjoy.

Nutrition:
Calories: 214
Fat: 3g
Cholesterol: 17mg
Carbs: 27g
Protein: 16g

128. Bacon-Wrapped Asparagus

Preparation Time: 15 minutes
Cooking Time: 30 min
Servings: 6
Ingredients:

- 15 - 20 spears of fresh asparagus (1 pound)
- Olive oil (extra virgin)
- 5 slices bacon (thinly sliced)
- 1 teaspoon salt and pepper (or your preferred rub)

Directions:

1. Break off the ends of the asparagus, then trim it all so they're down to the same length.
2. Separate the asparagus into bundles—3 spears per bundle. Then spritz them with some olive oil.
3. Use a piece of bacon to wrap up each bundle. When you're done, lightly dust the wrapped bundle with some salt and pepper to taste, or your preferred rub.
4. Put some fiberglass mats on your grates. Make sure they're the fiberglass kind. This will keep your asparagus from getting stuck on your grill gates.
5. Heat your smoker to 400°F. You can do this as you prep your asparagus.
6. Grill the wraps for 25 minutes to 30 minutes, tops. The goal is to get your asparagus looking nice and tender, and the bacon deliciously crispy.

Nutrition:
Calories: 71
Fat: 3g
Carbs: 1g
Protein: 6g

129. Garlic Parmesan Wedges

Preparation Time: 15 minutes
Cooking Time: 35 minutes
Servings: 3
Ingredients:

- 3 russet potatoes (large)
- 2 teaspoons of garlic powder
- ¾ teaspoon black pepper
- 1 ½ teaspoons of salt
- ¾ cup Parmesan cheese (grated)
- 3 tablespoons fresh cilantro (chopped, optional. You can replace this with flat-leaf parsley)
- ½ cup blue cheese (per serving, as optional dip. Can be replaced with ranch dressing)

Directions:

1. Use some cold water to scrub your potatoes as gently as you can with a veggie brush. When done, let them dry.
2. Slice your potatoes along the length in half. Cut each half into a third.
3. Get all the extra moisture off your potato by wiping it all away with a paper towel. If you don't do this, then you're not going to have crispy wedges!
4. In a large bowl, throw in your potato wedges, some olive oil, garlic powder, salt, garlic, and pepper, and then toss them with your hands, lightly. You want to make sure the spices and oil get on every wedge.
5. Place your wedges on a nonstick grilling tray, or pan, or basked. The single layer kind. Make sure it's at least 15 x 12 inches.
6. Heat your smoker to 425°F.
7. Set the grilling tray upon your Heated grill. Roast the wedges for 15 minutes before you flip them. Once you turn them, roast them for

another 15 minutes, or 20 tops. The outside should be a nice, crispy, golden brown.

8. Sprinkle your wedges generously with the Parmesan cheese. When you're done, garnish it with some parsley, or cilantro, if you like. Serve these bad boys up with some ranch dressing, or some blue cheese, or just eat them that way!

Nutrition:
Calories: 194
Fat: 5g
Cholesterol: 5mg
Carbs: 32g
Protein: 5g

130. Smoked Summer Vegetables
Preparation Time: 15 minutes
Cooking Time: 1 hour
Servings: 4
Ingredients:
- Summer squash
- 2 zucchini
- 1 onion
- 2 cups mushrooms
- 2 cups French-cut green beans

Directions:
1. Wash thoroughly and slice squash, onion, and zucchini, mushrooms, and green beans.
2. Combine all these ingredients and mix well.
3. Heat the electric smoker to 250F
4. Make 4 cup-shaped containers from heavy duty aluminum foil.
5. Put vegetables in these cups.
6. Add herbs and spices to taste.
7. Pinch the top of foil cups together.
8. Make several holes in the foil so that the smoke can circulate around the vegetables. Smoke for 1 hr. at 220F.

Nutrition:
Calories: 97
Protein: 5.6g
Carbs: 14g
Fat: 9g

131. Herby Smoked Cauliflower
Preparation Time: 20 minutes
Cooking Time: 2 hours
Servings: 4
Ingredients:
- 1 head cauliflower
- Olive oil
- Salt
- Pepper
- 2 tsps. dried oregano
- 2 tsps. Dried basil

Directions:
1. Start by soaking your wood chips for about an hour and Heating your smoker to 200°F/93°C.
2. Remove the wood chips from the liquid then pat dry before using.
3. Then take your cauliflower and chop into medium-sized pieces, removing the core.
4. Place the pieces of cauliflower onto a sheet pan and then drizzle with the olive oil.
5. Sprinkle the seasonings and herbs over the cauliflower then pop into the smoker.
6. Smoke for 2 hours, checking and turning often. Serve and enjoy!

Nutrition:
Calories: 31 Protein: 1.5g
Carbs: 6.7g Fat: 0.34g

132. Smoked Green Beans with Lemon

Preparation Time: 20 minutes
Cooking Time: 1 hour
Servings: 4
Ingredients:
- 2 lbs. fresh green beans, trimmed and soaked

- 2 tbsps. Apple vinaigrette dressing
- 1 lemon

Directions:
1. Place beans in a colander.
2. Heat smoker to 140°F and add wood chips (recommended Oak wood chips).
3. Put the beans in the pan in a single layer and lightly coat with the dressing.
4. Put the beans on the upper shelf of the smoker and smoke for 1 hour.
5. Remove from the heat, cover with foil and let rest for 15 minutes.
6. Pour lemon juice, sprinkle with the lemon zest and serve.

Nutrition:
Calories: 74.31
Total Fat: 0.66g
Total Carbs: 17.02g
Protein: 4.19g

133. Smoked Lemony-Garlic Artichokes

Preparation Time: 15 minutes
Cooking Time: 35 minutes
Servings: 4
Ingredients:
- 4 artichokes
- 4 minced garlic cloves
- 3 tbsps. Lemon juice
- ½ c. virgin olive oil
- 2 parsley sprigs
- Sea salt

Directions:
1. Put a large pot on your stove with a metal steaming basket inside.
2. Fill with water just to the bottom of the basket and bring to a boil.
3. Slice the artichoke tail and take out the toughest leaves.
4. With cooking shears, cut the pointy ends off of the outermost leaves.
5. Cut the artichokes in half lengthwise. Remove the hairy choke in the center.
6. Put the halves, stem side down, in the steamer basket. Reduce the heat to a rolling simmer.

7. On the pot, cover and steam for about 20 to 25 minutes, until the inside of the artichoke is tender.
8. Prepare a dressing: place in a mortar the garlic, lemon juice, olive oil, parsley, and salt.
9. Take away the basket and let the artichokes come to room temperature.
10. Heat your smoker to 200°F.
11. Place the artichokes in aluminum foil packets and brush garlic mixture all over the artichokes.
12. Smoke the artichokes halves for 1 hour.
13. Serve hot.

Nutrition:
Calories: 83.22 Total Fat: 0.29g
Total Carbs: 18.82g Protein: 5.54g

134. Smoked Portobello Mushrooms with Herbs de Provence

Preparation Time: 10 minutes
Cooking Time: 2 hours
Servings: 4
Ingredients:
- 12 large Portobello mushrooms
- 1 tbsp. Herbs de Provence
- ¼ c. extra virgin olive oil
- Sea salt
- Black pepper

Directions:
1. Heat smoker to 200°F and add wood chips (recommended oak wood chips).
2. In a bowl, mix Herbs de Provence, olive oil, salt, and pepper to taste.
3. Scrub the mushrooms with a dry cloth or paper towel.
4. Rub the mushrooms all over with herbs mixture.
5. Move the mushrooms, cap side down, directly on the top grill rack. Smoke for approximately 2 hours.
6. Move carefully so the herbal liquid in the cap remains in place.

Nutrition:
Calories: 146.08 Fat: 13.63g
Total Carbs: 5.22g Protein: 3.03g

135. Smoky Corn on the Cob

Preparation Time: 10 minutes
Cooking Time: 2 hours
Servings: 5
Ingredients:

- 10 ears sweet corn
- ½ c. butter
- Salt
- Black pepper

Directions:

1. Heat your smoker to 225°F and add wood chips (recommended oak or hickory).
2. Put the ears of corn on the top 2 racks of the smoker and smoke for 2 hours.
3. Rotate the corn every 30 minutes.
4. Serve hot with butter, salt, and pepper.

Nutrition:
Calories: 408.72
Total Fat: 22.27g
Total Carbs: 53.5g
Protein: 9.55g

136. Smoked Potato Salad

Preparation Time: 30 minutes
Cooking Time: 2 hours
Servings: 4
Ingredients:

- 3 eggs, hard-boiled
- 2 tbsps. cider vinegar
- 1 lb. russet potatoes
- 1 tbsp. Dijon mustard
- ½ c. red onion
- 1/3 c. light mayonnaise
- Salt
- Black pepper

Directions:

1. Heat the electric smoker to 225F.

2. Put prepared wood chips in the wood tray — use mesquite chips for the best result.
3. Put peeled potatoes in a saucepan and cover with water. Put on the lid and bring to a boil.
4. Cook for 20 mins. Pat potatoes dry, and put them on paper towels.
5. Directly smoke potatoes on the racks for 2 hrs. as you add extra wood chips in a cycle of 45 mins.
6. Remove potatoes, let them cool.
7. Chop them well for the preparation of the salad.
8. Combine boiled eggs, onion, mayonnaise, pickles, mustard, pepper, salt, and vinegar.
9. Mix all these ingredients well.
10. Add potatoes to the prepared mixture. Put in the fridge for several hrs. covered.

Nutrition:
Calories: 209
Total Fat: 9g
Total Carbs: 30g
Protein: 3g

137. Smoked Volcano Potatoes

Preparation Time: 15 minutes
Cooking Time: 1 hour
Servings: 2
Ingredients:

- 2 russet potatoes
- ¾ c. sour cream.
- 1 c. cheddar cheese
- 2 tbsps. green onion
- 8 bacon strips
- 4 tbsps. butter
- 2 tbsps. olive oil
- Salt

Directions:

1. Heat the electric smoker to 250F.
2. Wash potatoes, pierce using the fork.
3. Take the oil and salt and rub on the potatoes. Wrap the potatoes in foil and put in the smoker.
4. Smoke potatoes for 3 hrs.

5. Cut off the top of each potato and remove the potato flesh, leaving the shell empty.
6. Fry and crumble the bacon. Combine potato flesh with bacon, butter, sour cream, and cheese in a bowl.
7. Put the prepared filling in the potatoes, add some cheese on the top.
8. Wrap the potato with 2 bacon slices — for securing use toothpicks.
9. Smoke for another 1 hr.
10. Add green onions with a little sour cream on top (sour cream will give a special flavor to the potato).

Nutrition:
Calories: 256
Total Fat: 39.3g
Total Carbs: 31.7g
Protein: 32.1g

138. Groovy Smoked Asparagus
Preparation Time: 5 minutes
Cooking Time: 90 minutes
Servings: 4
Ingredients:

- 1 bunch asparagus
- 2 tbsps. Olive oil
- 1 tsp. chopped garlic
- Kosher salt
- ½ tsp. black pepper

Directions:
1. Prepare the water pan of your smoker accordingly
2. Pre-heat your smoker to 275 degrees Fahrenheit/135 degree Celsius
3. Fill a medium-sized bowl with water and add 3-4 handfuls of woods and allow them to soak
4. Add the asparagus to a grill basket in a single layer
5. Drizzle olive oil on top and sprinkle garlic, pepper, and salt
6. Toss them well
7. Put the basket in your smoker
8. Add a few chips into the loading bay and keep repeating until all of the chips after every 20 minutes

9. Smoke for 60-90 minutes
10. Serve and enjoy!

Nutrition:
Calories: 68
Total Fat: 4.1g
Total Carbs: 7.1g
Protein: 2.8g

139. Smoked Squash Casserole
Preparation Time: 40 minutes
Cooking Time: 1 hour 15 minutes
Servings: 3
Ingredients:

- 2½ lbs. yellow squash
- 2 tbsps. parsley flakes
- 2 eggs, beaten
- 1 medium yellow onion
- 1 sleeve saltine crackers
- 1 package Velveeta cheese
- ½ c. Alouette Sun-dried Tomato
- Basil cheese spread
- ¼ c. Alouette Garlic and Herb cheese spread
- ¼ c. mayonnaise
- ¾ tsp. hot sauce
- ¼ tsp. Cajun seasoning
- ½ c. butter
- ¼ tsp. salt
- ¼ tsp. black pepper

Directions:
1. Heat the electric smoker to 250F.
2. Combine squash and onion in a saucepan and add water to cover. Boil on medium heat until tender.
3. Drain and to this hot mixture, add Velveeta cheese, Alouette cheese, mayonnaise, parsley flakes, hot sauce, Cajun seasoning, salt, and pepper to taste.
4. Stir all together well.
5. Cool a little, add eggs and stir until mixed.
6. Melt butter in a saucepan.
7. Add crushed crackers to the butter and stir well. Combine ½ cup of butter-cracker mix with the squash mixture. Stir thoroughly.
8. Pour into a disposable aluminum foil pan. Top the squash with

remaining butter and crackers. Cover the pan tightly with aluminum foil.

9. Put on the lower rack of the smoker and cook for 1 hr. Put one small handful of prepared wood chips in the wood tray for the best result use hickory.
10. For an hour, remove the foil from the casserole and cook for another 15 mins.

Nutrition:
Calories: 190Total Fat: 8g
Total Carbs: 23g Protein: 7g

140. Smoked Eggplant

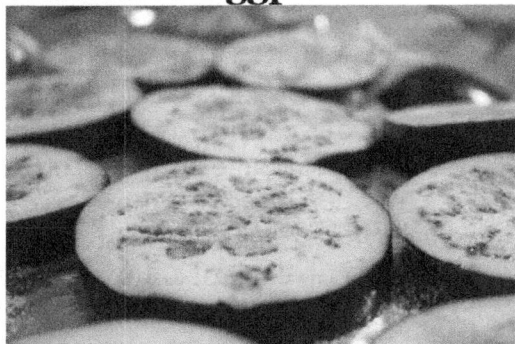

Preparation Time: 20 minutes
Cooking Time: 1 hour
Servings: 4
Ingredients:
- 2 medium eggplant
- Olive oil

Directions:
1. Heat your smoker to 200°F and soak your wood chips for an hour.
2. Remove the wood chips from the liquid then pat dry before using.
3. Then carefully peel your eggplant then slice into rounds of around ¼"/1cm thick.
4. Brush each of these rounds with olive oil then place directly into the smoker.
5. Smoke for approximately an hour until soft and tender. Serve and enjoy!

Nutrition:
Calories: 85
Protein: 1.6g
Carbs: 9.4g
Fat: 4.6g

141. Twice Pulled Potatoes
Preparation Time: 30 minutes
Cooking Time: 2 hours 40 minutes
Servings: 4
Ingredients:
- 1 lb. pulled pork
- 2 russet potatoes
- 1/3 c. sour cream
- 4 oz. cream cheese
- 1/3 c. cheddar cheese
- Chives
- BBQ sauce, to taste

Directions:
1. Heat the electric smoker to 225F. Smoke washed potatoes for 2 hours.
2. Mix potato flesh, cheddar cheese, sour cream, cream cheese, pulled pork and BBQ sauce in a bowl and stir well.
3. Put prepared mixture back into potatoes skins.
4. Smoke for another 40 mins.
5. Season with more BBQ sauce, if desired. Sprinkle some cheddar cheese and chives on the top.

Nutrition:
Calories: 285
Protein: 3g
Carbs: 24.1g
Fat: 8.1g

142. Smoked Apple Crumble
Preparation Time: 10 minutes
Cooking Time: 1 hour
Servings: 15
Ingredients:
For the pie filling:
- 3 tsps. All-purpose flour
- 1 tsp. ground cinnamon
- 1 c. sugar
- 3 lbs. apples
For crumble:
- 2 c. rolled oats
- ½ tsp. baking powder
- ½ tsp. baking soda
- 1 c. butter
- 2 c. brown sugar
- Ice cream to serve

Directions:

1. Heat the smoker to 275°F following the manufacturer's instructions.
2. Make the pie filling as follows: Mix together in a bowl all the pie-filling ingredients and toss well.
3. Transfer into 14-15 ramekins (2/3 fill it). Do not grease the ramekins.
4. To make crumble: Mix together in a bowl flour, brown sugar, oats, baking powder and baking soda. Pour butter over it and mix well.
5. Place about ¼ cup of this mixture over each of the ramekins (over the apple filling). Place the ramekins on the center rack in the smoker and smoke for an hour.
6. Remove the ramekins from the smoker and invert onto individual serving bowls. Serve as it is or with a scoop of ice cream.

Nutrition:
Calories: 267
Protein: 2.6g
Carbs: 41.4g
Fat: 13.3g

143. Smoked Coleslaw

Preparation Time: 1 hour 10 minutes
Cooking Time: 30 minutes
Servings: 10 - 12
Ingredients:

- 1 head cabbage, shredded
- 1 carrot, shredded
- ¼ cup sugar
- ½ teaspoon salt
- ½ teaspoon freshly ground black pepper
- ¼ cup white vinegar

- 1 cup heavy whip cream
- 1 teaspoon paprika

Directions:

1. Heat the smoker to 175°F with the maple wood.
2. Spread the cabbage and carrot in a shallow aluminum foil pan. Place the pan in the smoker then smoke the vegetables for 30 minutes. Remove from the smoker and transfer the vegetables to a large bowl.
3. Stir in the sugar, salt, pepper, vinegar, and heavy cream to combine. Refrigerate for 1 hour before serving.
4. Sprinkle with paprika.
5. VARIATION TIP: This sweet dressing is also excellent for a broccoli-cauliflower salad. Instead of the cabbage and carrot, use 2 cups each of chopped broccoli, cauliflower, and cooked bacon, and add 1 cup each of chopped scallions (white and green parts) and celery.

Nutrition:
Calories 69
Total Fat 3.8g
Saturated Fat 2.3g
Cholesterol 14mg
Sodium 115mg
Total Carbohydrate 8.6g
Dietary Fiber 1.7g
Total Sugars 6.4g
Protein 1.1g
Vitamin D 5mcg
Calcium 33mg
Iron 0mg
Potassium 134mg

144. Smoked Onion Bombs
Preparation Time: 15 minutes
Cooking Time: 2 hours
Servings: 4
Ingredients:

- 4 large Vidalia onions, peeled
- ½ cup (1 stick) butter, divided
- 4 chicken bouillon cubes
- ½ cup grated Parmesan cheese

- 1 teaspoon freshly ground black pepper

Directions:
1. Heat the smoker to 225F with the maple or mesquite wood.
2. Angle a sharp knife into the onion from the top and cut all the way around, removing the top and creating a deep well in the onion. Repeat with the remaining onions. Save the onion tops.
3. Place four pieces of aluminum foil, each about 8 inches square. Place each onion on a sheet of foil. Press 2 tablespoons of butter into the well of each onion and top with a bouillon cube.
4. Mix the Parmesan and pepper. Place 2 tablespoons of the mixture in each onion well.
5. Replace the onion tops tightly (cutting as necessary to fit) and wrap the foil up the sides, but leave the top of the packet open to allow the smoke flavor to permeate the onions.
6. Smoke the onions for about 2 hours, until tender.
7. INGREDIENT TIP: When shopping in the produce section, look for firm bulbs with no bruises or soft areas. Onions can be kept in the refrigerator's crisper drawer, but avoid storing in plastic bags, as the onions are then prone to develop mold.

Nutrition:
Total Fat 24.3g
Saturated Fat 15.3g
Cholesterol 64mg
Sodium 814mg
Total Carbohydrate 15.4g
Dietary Fiber 3.4g
Total Sugars 7g
Protein 3.6g
Vitamin D 16mcg
Calcium 77mg
Iron 1mg
Potassium 249mg

145. Smoked Cabbage
Preparation Time: 10 minutes
Cooking Time: 2 hours
Servings: 4
Ingredients:
- 1 head cabbage, cored completely
- 4 tablespoons butter
- 2 tablespoons rendered bacon fat, or 2 more tablespoons butter, melted
- 1 chicken bouillon cube
- 1 teaspoon freshly ground black pepper
- 1 garlic clove, minced

Directions:
1. Heat the smoker to 240°F with the apple, maple, or oak wood.
2. Fill the hole left by coring the cabbage with the butter, bacon fat, bouillon cube, pepper, and garlic.
3. Wrap the cabbage in aluminum foil, two-thirds of the way up the sides to protect the outer leaves, leaving the top open to allow the smoke flavor to permeate the cabbage. Place the cabbage on the grill rack and smoke for about 2 hours.
4. Unwrap and enjoy as a side dish.

Nutrition:
Calories 202Total Fat 17.6g
Saturated Fat 11.1g
Cholesterol 46mg
Sodium 268mg
Total Carbohydrate 11.2g
Dietary Fiber 4.6g
Total Sugars 5.9g
Protein 2.7g
Vitamin D 8mcg
Calcium 81mg
Iron 1mg Potassium 322mg

146. Loaded Hasselback Potatoes
Preparation Time: 20 minutes
Cooking Time: 1 hour 30 minutes
Servings: 4
Ingredients:
- 4 russet potatoes, cut Hasselback style (slice into the potato, all the way across, making your cuts about

¼ inch apart and being careful not to cut all the way through the bottom of the potato)

- 1 cup olive oil, divided
- 2 teaspoons salt
- 2 teaspoons freshly ground black pepper
- 1 small onion, sliced
- 2 jalapeño peppers, seeded and thinly sliced
- 2 cherry peppers, sliced
- 4 ounces block Cheddar cheese, thickly sliced
- 8 bacon slices, cooked and crumbled

Directions:

1. Heat the smoker to 250°F with the hickory wood.
2. Place the potatoes on a grill pan. Drizzle ½ cup of olive oil over the potatoes and sprinkle with the salt and pepper. Move the pan in the smoker and smoke for about 1 hour.
3. Take off the potatoes from the smoker and place some onion, jalapeños, cherry peppers, Cheddar slices, and crumbled bacon in between each potato slice and on top.
4. Pour the remaining ½ cup of olive oil over all. Return the potatoes to the smoker for 30 to 40 minutes or so, until the potatoes are tender in a squeeze test.
5. Serve with sour cream, if desired.

Nutrition:

Calories 2085
Total Fat 166.3g
Saturated Fat 48.2g
Cholesterol 309mg
Sodium 7644mg
Total Carbohydrate 41.3g
Dietary Fiber 6.1g
Total Sugars 3.6g
Protein 105.1g
Vitamin D 3mcg
Calcium 263mg
Iron 6mg
Potassium 2390mg

147. Garlic-Rosemary Potato Wedges

Preparation Time: 15 minutes
Cooking Time: 1 hour 30 minutes
Servings: 6 – 8
Ingredients:

- 4 to 6 large russet potatoes, cut into wedges
- ¼ cup olive oil
- 2 garlic cloves, minced
- 1 tablespoon dried rosemary
- 2 teaspoons salt
- 1 teaspoon freshly ground black pepper
- 1 teaspoon sugar
- 1 teaspoon onion powder

Directions:

1. Heat the smoker to 250°F with the maple or pecan wood.
2. Toss the potatoes with the olive oil to coat them well.
3. Stir together the garlic, rosemary, salt, pepper, sugar, and onion powder. Season this mixture on all sides of the potato wedges. Transfer the seasoned wedges to a grill pan and put it into the smoker.
4. Cook for about 1½ hours until a fork cuts through the wedges easily.

Nutrition:

Calories 377 Total Fat 13.3g
Saturated Fat 2g Cholesterol 0mg
Sodium 1187mg
Total Carbohydrate 61.4g
Dietary Fiber 9.8g
Total Sugars 5.5g
Protein 6.5g Vitamin D 0mcg
Calcium 62mg
Iron 3mg
Potassium 1536mg

148. Smoked Asparagus

Preparation Time: 10 minutes
Cooking Time: 1 hour
Servings: 4 - 5
Ingredients:

- 2 tablespoons butter, melted
- 2 garlic cloves, minced
- 2 tablespoons freshly squeezed lemon juice
- 1 tablespoon capers
- 1 tablespoon onion powder
- 1 teaspoon salt
- ½ teaspoon freshly ground black pepper
- 1 pound asparagus (about 18 to 20 stalks), woody ends snapped off

Directions:

1. Heat the smoker to 240°F with the maple wood.
2. Stir together the butter, garlic, lemon juice, capers, onion powder, salt, and pepper.
3. Cook the asparagus in a grill pan and drizzle with the seasoned butter. Put the pan in the smoker and smoke for about 1 hour until tender.

Nutrition:
Calories 68 Total Fat 4.8g
Saturated Fat 3g Cholesterol 12mg
Sodium 555mg
Total Carbohydrate 5.4g
Dietary Fiber 2.2g
Total Sugars 2.4g
Protein 2.4g
Vitamin D 3mcg
Calcium 33mg
Iron 2mg
Potassium 213mg

149. Smoked Bacon-Wrapped Onion Rings

Preparation Time: 20 minutes
Cooking Time: 1 hour 30 minutes
Servings: 16 onion rings
Ingredients:

- 2 large onions, peeled and sliced ½ inch thick (about 4 slices from each onion)
- ¼ cup hot sauce
- 4 tablespoons butter, melted
- 1 pound bacon
- 1 tablespoon cayenne pepper
- 1 tablespoon sugar

Directions:

1. Heat the smoker to 250°F with the hickory, maple, or mesquite wood.
2. Separate the onion rings and remove the smaller internal rings to save for another use. I recommend leaving two rings intact on each to keep them sturdy. You should get about eight rings out of one large onion, two out of each slice.
3. Mix the hot sauce and melted butter.
4. Dip the onion rings in the butter–hot sauce mixture.
5. Wrap each onion ring tightly with a bacon slice.
6. In another small bowl, stir together the cayenne and sugar. Coat the bacon-wrapped rings well with this mixture. Secure the rings with toothpicks or place them on skewers.
7. Place the onion rings on a grill mat and smoke for about 1½ hours until the bacon is done and beyond "chewy" to bite through.

Nutrition:
Calories 254
Total Fat 19.8g
Saturated Fat 7.6g
Cholesterol 52mg
Sodium 1028mg
Total Carbohydrate 4.2g
Dietary Fiber 0.7g
Total Sugars 2.2g
Protein 14.4g
Vitamin D 3mcg
Calcium 12mg
Iron 1mg
Potassium 267mg

150. Smoked Artichokes

Preparation Time: 5 minutes
Cooking Time: 2 hours
Servings: 8
Ingredients:

- ¼ cup olive oil
- 1 garlic clove, minced
- 1 teaspoon salt
- Juice of 1 lemon
- 4 artichokes, stemmed and halved lengthwise

Directions:

1. Pre-heat the smoker to 225°F with the hickory or maple wood.
2. Whisk together the garlic, olive oil, salt, and lemon juice.
3. Brush the artichoke halves with the seasoned olive oil. Place them directly on the smoker's grate and smoke for about 2 hours. The artichoke bottoms should look and feel tender when poked with a fork.

Nutrition:
Calories 94
Total Fat 6.5g
Saturated Fat 1g
Cholesterol 0mg
Sodium 368mg
Total Carbohydrate 8.7g
Dietary Fiber 4.4g
Total Sugars 0.9g
Protein 2.7g
Vitamin D 0mcg
Calcium 37mg
Iron 1mg
Potassium 306mg

151. Hasselback Sweet Potatoes

Preparation Time: 15 minutes
Cooking Time: 1 hour 30 minutes
Servings: 4 - 6
Ingredients:

- 4 large sweet potatoes, scrubbed
- ¼ cup canola oil
- 2 tablespoons table salt
- ½ cup (1 stick) butter
- 4 serrano peppers, seeded and sliced
- 1 cup Glazed Spiced Pecans (here), coarsely chopped
- 1 tablespoon sea salt
- ¼ cup honey

Directions:

1. Heat the smoker to 250°F with the pecan wood.
2. Rub the sweet potatoes all over with the oil and table salt.
3. Cut them thick-sliced Hasselback-style: Slice into the sweet potatoes, all the way across, making your cuts about ½ inch apart, and being careful not to cut all the way through the bottom of the sweet potato (see tip).
4. Place the sweet potatoes on a grill pan and put it into the smoker. Smoke for 1 hour, then remove from the heat.
5. Place a pat of butter between each slice.
6. Stuff serrano slices and pecans between the slices.
7. Sprinkle well with the sea salt and drizzle with the honey, getting it between the slices.
8. Smoke for 30 to 40 minutes more and remove from the smoker when the potatoes pass the squeeze test.

Nutrition:
Calories 434 Total Fat 38.3g
Saturated Fat 11.7g Cholesterol 41mg
Sodium 3446mg
Total Carbohydrate 24.3g Dietary Fiber 2.8g
Total Sugars 12.9g Protein 2.8g
Vitamin D 11mcg Calcium 24mg
Iron 1mg Potassium 261mg

CHAPTER 9:

Cheese and Nuts Recipes

152. Smoking Hard and Semi-hard Cheeses

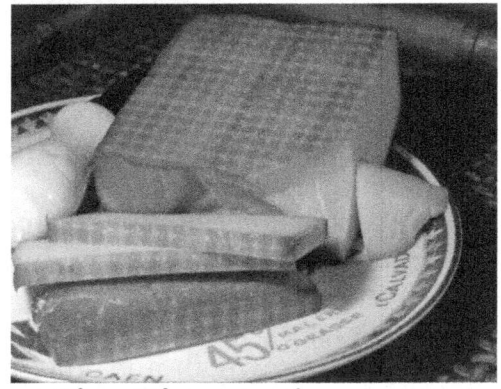

Preparation Time: 5 min
Cooking time: 2 to 4 hour
Servings: 14 people
Ingredients:
- 4 eight ounce blocks of cheese
- sharp cheddar
- Manchego
- Gruyere
- halloumi, or all four

Directions:
1. Keep the cheese refrigerated while setting up your smoker. Preheat your smoker to between 75°F and 85°F with the vent open. Place wood chips in the side tray and cold water in the bowl.
2. Place the blocks of cold cheese on a mesh wire rack and place that on a rack inside the smoker. Alternatively, place the cheese directly on the smoker rack. Cold smoke for 2 hours, turning over once or twice. Check for a slight bronze color and taste to see if the cheese has adequate smoke flavor. Continue to smoke for up to 4 hours if desired.

3. Remove the smoked cheese from the smoker and allow it to rest on a rack for approximately 1 hour. If there is a film of oil on the cheese you can blot that off with a paper towel. When the cheese has rested, seal it in plastic wrap or butcher's paper. Place this in the cheese drawer of your refrigerator and leave alone for approximately 7 days for the smoke flavor to mature.

Nutrition:
Calories: 198
Fat: 17g
Cholesterol: 48mg
Carbs: 3g
Protein: 8g

153. Jalapeño Bacon Smoked Mac & Cheese

Preparation time: $1^{1/2}$ hour
Cooking time: 2 hour
Serving: 4
Ingredients:
- 450 g macaroni 450 g bacon
- 1 jalapeño
- 1 cup shredded sharp cheddar cheese
- 1 cup shredded mild cheddar cheese
- ¼ cup shredded parmesan cheese
- 4 Tbsp butter
- 4 Tbsp all-purpose flour
- 1 cup milk
- 1 cup heavy whipping cream
- Salt and pepper to taste

Directions:
1. Preheat smoker to 175°C (propane) or 135°C (electric).

2. Boil macaroni in a large pot. Drain water and set aside.

3. Dice and brown the bacon. Set aside.

4. In the same large pot, on medium heat, melt butter then stir in flour. Add salt and pepper to taste.

5. Keep whisking/stirring to keep roux from clumping. Whisk in milk, when combined with the roux – whisk in heavy whipping cream.

6. Keep whisking and add cheeses one at a time, adding the next as the previous one starts to melt. Continue to whisk until sauce is completely melted.

7. Remove from heat and add in bacon, jalapeños, and macaroni. Stir until thoroughly mixed.

8. Put the mac and cheese in an aluminum tray. Smoke for 45 minutes at 175°C (propane) and 1 hr. at 135°C (electric).

9. Serve and enjoy!

Nutrition:
Calories: 25 Cal
Carbs: 0 g
Fat: 2 g
Protein: 4 g
Fiber: 0 g.

154. Smoked Cauliflower Mac N Cheese

Preparation Time: 10 mins
Cooking Time: 1 hour
Servings: 6-8
Ingredients:

- 1 head cauliflower, chopped (equivalent to 3 cups)
- 1 cup grated cheddar cheese
- ½ heavy cream
- 3 tbsp. grated pork rinds (MSG free)
- 1 tsp sea salt
- 1 tsp fresh ground pepper
- 1 tsp smoked paprika
- Chopped green onions (optional)

Directions:

1. Steam cauliflower until barely fork tender.

2. While steaming, make the cheese sauce by simmering the cream on low and adding the cheese stirring to melt, about 10 minutes. Add in the salt, pepper and smoked paprika.

3. Evenly spread the cauliflower in a 12-inch cast iron skillet and cover with the sauce.

4. Place the skillet in the smoker with oak or pecan and smoke for 30 minutes at 250 degrees on indirect heat to obtain smoke flavor.

5. After smoking for 30 minutes, crank the heat up on the Smoker to 350 degrees, with the cast iron still on indirect heat.

6. Sprinkle the cauliflower mac and cheese with the bacon bits and ground up pork rinds.

7. Cook for 25-30 minutes or until the top is browned and the cheese mixture has begun to bubble.

8. Remove from oven, garnish with chopped green onion, let cool for 10 minutes and serve immediately.

Nutrition:
Calories 770
Total Fat 29.2g
Saturated Fat 1.7g
Cholesterol 249mg
Sodium 9583mg
Total Carbohydrate 47.8g

155. Smoked Mac 'N' Cheese

Preparation Time: 30 minutes
Cooking Time: 60 minutes
Servings: 6
Ingredients:

- 1 450 g (3,20 lbs.) elbow macaroni
- ¼ cup butter

- ¼ cup all-purpose flour
- 3 cups milk
- 1 (220 g, 0,5lb.) cream cheese, cut into large chunks
- 1 tsp salt
- ½ tsp black pepper
- 2 cups (220 g, 0,5lb.) extra sharp Cheddar cheese, shredded
- 2 cups (220 g, 0,5lb.) Gouda cheese, shredded
- 1 cup (110 g, 0,25lb.) Parmesan cheese, shredded
- Optional: pulled pork, bacon, brisket.

Directions:
1. Load the wood tray with one small handful of wood chips and preheat the smoker to 110°C.
2. Cook pasta according to package directions. In a medium saucepan, melt butter, and whisk flour into the butter. Cook over medium heat for 2 minutes, until sauce is bubbly and thick. Whisk in milk and bring to a boil. Cook 5 minutes until thickened. Stir in cream cheese until mixture is smooth. Add salt and pepper.
3. In a large bowl, combine 1 cup Cheddar, 1 cup Gouda cheese, Parmesan cheese, pasta, cream sauce, and optional ingredients. Spoon mixture into an aluminum roasting pan coated with nonstick cooking spray. Sprinkle top with remaining Cheddar cheese and Gouda cheese.
4. Place in smoker and cook 1 hour at 110°C, until brown, bubbly and delicious.

Nutrition:
Calories: 678.8 Fat: 61.1 g
Protein: 30.2 g Carbs: 0.6 g

156. Easy Cold Smoked Cheese
Preparation time: 30 minutes
Cooking Time: 2 hours
Servings: 8
Ingredients:
- 1 Smoke tube

- 1 Applewood
- 1 Grill surface thermometer
- 1 Parchment paper
- 8 lbs cheese Gouda or mild cheddar

Directions:
1. Set up smoker to cold smoke, using either a tube smoker or cold smoke generator. Add applewood. Use a grill surface thermometer to ensure temperature does not exceed 80°F or 26°C.
2. Place cheese blocks on smoker grates. Close lid and leave for 2 hours. Turn cheese over every 30 minutes.
3. Remove cheese from smoker and wrap in parchment paper. Avoid wrapping too tightly, and allow cheese to breathe.
4. Transfer cheese to refrigerator and leave for 24 hours. Unwrap and transfer to vacuum sealed bag. Leave to rest in refrigerator for 1-2 weeks. The longer you leave the cheese, the better the taste will be.

Nutrition:
Calories: 60 Cal
Carbs: 0 g
Fat: 2 g,
Protein: 10 g
Fiber: 0 g.

157. Smoked Seed And Nut
Preparation time: 3 hours
Cooking Time: 45 minutes
Servings: 4
Ingredients:
- ½ Gallons water
- ½ Cup kosher salt
- Quart Zip lock bags
- favorite seasonings
- Spray Cooking Oil
- 1/2 tbsp. melted butter

Directions:
1. For the brine, stir 1/2 gallon of water and 1/2 cup of kosher salt together.
2. Place your nuts or seeds in individual sealable plastic bags and swill with the brine.

3. Let sit on a flat surface for two hours.
4. Drain the brine and place nuts and seeds in a bowl. Liberally spray with cooking oil, pour in your favorite seasoning and mix it up.
5. Make sure all nuts and seeds are coated in oil and seasoning.
6. Place nuts and/or seeds flat in a foil pan.
7. Wrap your smoker shelves with foil and lay the nuts and/or seeds across the shelves.
8. Add enough wood chips for about 2 hours of smoke.
9. Set it to 230°F; other electric smoker models will vary on if/how you set the cooker temperature,
10. Be done in about 2 hours. Nuts need longer to roast, but you only need about 2 hours of smoke to infuse the flavor.
11. Leave nuts in the smoker for an additional 2 to 3 hours, depending on the type of nuts.
12. For pecans, almonds and pumpkin seeds: smoke for two hours and cook for two hours, totaling four hours at 230°F.
13. For peanuts, smoke for two hours and cook for three hours, totaling five hours at 230°F. Peanuts will remain soft until they've cooled.

Nutrition:
Calcium, Ca36 mg
Magnesium, Mg35 mg
Phosphorus, P53 mg
Iron, Fe0.46 mg
Potassium, K112 mg
Sodium, Na589 mg

158. Smoked Almond Nut
Preparation time: 2 hours
Cooking Time: 2 hours
Servings: 8
Ingredients:
- 1 pound almonds , raw
- 2 tbsp butter , melted
- 1 tbsp salt
- 1 tsp garlic powder

- 1/2 tsp cayenne pepper

Directions:
1. Set up smoker for 250F using wood chips of choice. I usually use hickory when smoking nuts.
2. Mix together the melted butter, salt, garlic powder and cayenne pepper in a medium sized bowl. Stir in the almonds ensuring they are evenly coated.
3. Line smoker rack with aluminum foil and spread almonds evenly across the foil.
4. Smoke for about 2 hours.
5. Let the almonds cool completely and come to room temperature before serving.

Nutrition:
Calories: 190
Total Fat: 8g
Total Carbs: 23g
Protein: 7g

159. Sweet and Spicy BBQ Smoked Pecans
Preparation Time: 15 minutes
Cooking Time: 45
Servings: 8-10
Ingredients:
- 3 cups pecans

BBQ Rub
- 1 tablespoon smoked sugar OR brown sugar
- 1 tablespoon smoked paprika
- tablespoon smoked sea salt
- 1 tablespoon smoked coarsely ground black pepper
- ½ tablespoon ground coriander
- 1/2 tablespoon chipotle powder
- 1 teaspoon brown sugar

Directions:
1. Soak nuts in water for 10 minutes, then remove and lightly pat dry (getting the nuts wet helps the smoke adhere to their surface).
2. Combine the rub ingredients in a large bowl.
3. Toss the nuts in the rub so that all the nuts are covered in seasoning.

4. Place the nuts on a frog mat and smoke for 45 minutes to an hour until the nuts have begun to lightly brown.

Nutrition:
Calories: 25 Cal
Carbs: 0 g
Fat: 2 g
Protein: 4 g
Fiber: 0 g.

160. Hickory Smoked Mixed Nuts

Preparation Time: 10 minutes
Cooking Time: 50 minutes
Servings: 10
Ingredients:
- 1 lb Mixed Nuts (salted or unsalted)
- 4 tsp Melted Butter
- 1/4 Cup Brown Sugar
- 1/4 Cup White Sugar
- 1 tsp Garlic Powder
- 3/4 tsp Cayenne Pepper
- 1 tsp Salt (if your nuts are unsalted)

Directions:
1. Prepare your smoker and bring the temperature up to 235-245 degrees F. You can use any wood chips you like, I used hickory wood chips and they turned out fantastic!
2. In a medium bowl, mix together the melted butter, brown sugar, white sugar, garlic powder, cayenne pepper and salt if needed.
3. Toss in the mixed nuts and stir to make sure that they are all coated. Pour the nut mixture on to the slotted foil pan and place nuts in the smoker.

4. After 1 hour stir the nuts or mix them by shaking the pan. Return the pan to the smoker and allow them to smoke for the remaining hour.

Nutrition:
Calories: 332
Fat: 27g
Saturated Fat: 6g
Trans Fat: 0g
Unsaturated Fat: 20g
Cholesterol: 11mg
Sodium: 818mg
Carbohydrates: 20g
Fiber: 4g
Sugar: 11g
Protein: 8g

161. Cinnamon Smoked Almonds
Preparation time: 10 minutes
Cooking Time: 1 hour
Servings: 8
Ingredients:
- 1 pound raw, unsalted almond
- 1 egg white
- 2 teaspoons vanilla extract
- 1 cup light brown sugar
- 1 teaspoon ground nutmeg
- 1 teaspoon cinnamon
- ¾ teaspoon kosher salt
- ¼ teaspoon ground ginger

Directions:
1. Preheat your smoker to 225 degrees F using a mild wood like maple, pecan, or alder.
2. In a large mixing bowl, whisk the egg white until frothy. Mix in the 2 teaspoons vanilla extract.
3. In a smaller bowl, combine the brown sugar, salt, cinnamon, ginger, and nutmeg. Stir until the ingredients are evenly incorporated.
4. Pour the almonds into the egg white mixture and gently stir until the almonds are all evenly coated.
5. Pour the cinnamon sugar mixture over the almonds and stir again.
6. Once the almonds are covered in the sugar mixture, pour them onto

a parchment lined cookie sheet that has been lightly coated in cooking spray. Spread the almonds into a single layer.

7. Place in your smoker and cook for 1 hour, or until the almonds are no longer sticky (this could take an extra 15-20 minutes, depending on your smoker). Remove them from the heat and allow them to cool slightly before breaking them up and enjoying them.

8. Make sure the almonds are completely cooled before transferring to any lidded or sealed container.

Nutrition:
Calories: 436kcal
Carbohydrates: 39g
Protein: 12g
Fat: 28g
Saturated Fat: 2g
Sodium: 232mg
Potassium: 442mg
Fiber: 7g
Sugar: 29g
Calcium: 175mg
Iron: 2.3mg

162. Smoked Maple Walnuts
Preparation time: 10 mins
Cooking Time: 3 hrs.
Serving: 12
Ingredients:
- 4 cups raw walnut halves
- 1/4 cup butter or ghee
- 1/2 cup real maple syrup
- Coarse Kosher salt to taste

Directions:
1. Preheat the smoke to 275° and get the smoker filled with smoke.
2. Melt butter or ghee
3. Stir in real maple syrup until blended.
4. Pour over nuts and toss to mix.
5. Add to an aluminum pan. Generously sprinkle with salt.
6. Smoke for 3-5 hours.
7. Allow to cool completely to bring out the full smoke flavor.
8. Store in an air tight container for up to a week.

Nutrition:
Calories: 678.8
Fat: 61.1 g
Protein: 30.2 g
Carbs: 0.6 g

CHAPTER 10:

Rubs, Sauces, Marinades, And Dips

163. BBQ Sauce for Chicken

Preparation Time: 5 minutes
Cooking Time: 5-8 minutes
Servings: 1 ½-2 cups
Ingredients:

- 1 cup ketchup
- ¼ cup brown sugar
- ¼ cup apple cider vinegar
- 2 tablespoons smoked paprika
- 1 tablespoon extra-virgin olive oil
- 1 tablespoon chili powder
- 2 teaspoons garlic powder
- ½ teaspoon salt

Directions:

1. Combine the ingredients together in a saucepan.
2. Place on the stove and heat on medium.
3. Light boil and simmer for 5-8 minutes to blend the flavors.
4. Cool before storing in the fridge, covered, for no longer than a week.

Nutrition:
Total calories: 126
Protein: 1.1
Carbs: 24.1
Fat: 3.7
Fiber: 0.2

164. BBQ Sauce for Beef
Preparation Time: 5 minutes
Cooking Time: 35 minutes
Servings: 2 ½ cups
Ingredients:

- 3 tablespoons extra-virgin olive oil
- 1 cup diced onion
- 3 minced garlic cloves
- 1 ½ cups tomato sauce
- ¾ cup pure maple syrup
- ½ cup beef stock
- ½ cup apple cider vinegar
- 3 tablespoons chipotle chili powder
- 2 tablespoons Worcestershire sauce
- ½ teaspoon salt

Directions:

1. Heat a saucepan and add oil.
2. When hot, cook onion and garlic until softened.
3. Add the rest of the ingredients and bring to a boil.
4. Reduce heat and simmer for 30 minutes.
5. Cool before using, and store extra in a covered container in the fridge for up to a week.

Nutrition:
Total calories: 235 Protein: 1.5
Carbs: 39.2
Fat: 8.7
Fiber: 1.6

165. Mustard Sauce for Pork
Preparation Time: 5 minutes
Cooking Time: 27 minutes
Servings: 4 cups
Ingredients:

- 1 cup yellow mustard
- ½ cup balsamic vinegar

- 1/3 cup brown sugar
- 2 tablespoons butter
- 1 tablespoon fresh lemon juice
- 2 teaspoons Worcestershire sauce
- ½ teaspoon chili powder

Directions:
1. Put all the ingredients in a saucepan.
2. Heat until simmering, stirring.
3. Reduce the heat to low after 1-2 minutes of a light boil, then simmer for 25 minutes.
4. Cool to room-temperature before storing for 3-4 days in the fridge, or use right away!

Nutrition:
Total calories: 148
Protein: 2.8
Carbs: 16
Fat: 8.3
Fiber: 2.1

166. Spicy-Citrus Cocktail Sauce
Preparation Time: 5 minutes
Cooking Time: 6 minutes
Servings: 1 ¼ cups
Ingredients:

- 1 cup ketchup
- ¼ cup orange juice
- 1 minced chipotle chile
- 2 tablespoons diced onion
- 1 tablespoon Worcestershire sauce
- 2 teaspoons adobo sauce
- 2 teaspoons dry cilantro
- 1 teaspoon orange zest
- Pinch of red pepper flakes (or more)

Directions:
1. Prepare the ingredients in a saucepan then heat on medium.
2. When simmering, reduce heat, so sauce is barely bubbling.
3. Cook for 5-6 minutes, to blend flavors.
4. Let it rest to room temperature before storing in the fridge.
5. You can serve cocktail sauce cold or warm.

Nutrition:

Total calories: 58
Protein: 0.9
Carbs: 14.6
Fat: 0.2
Fiber: 0.2

167. Brisket Dry Rub
Preparation Time: 5 minutes
Cooking Time: Overnight
Servings: 1
Ingredients:

- ½ cup onion powder
- ¼ cup salt
- ¼ cup sweet paprika
- ¼ cup brown sugar
- ½ cup black pepper
- ½ cup garlic powder

Directions:
1. Mix all the seasonings together.
2. Rub on your brisket!
3. For best results, let the seasoned brisket sit in the fridge, covered, overnight.

Nutrition:
Total calories: 23
Protein: 0
Carbs: 5.9
Fat: 0
Fiber: 0

168. Pork Dry Rub
Preparation Time: 5 minutes
Cooking Time: Overnight
Servings: 3- 4
Ingredients:

- 1 cup brown sugar
- 3 tablespoons smoked paprika
- 1 tablespoon chili powder
- 2 teaspoons garlic powder
- 2 teaspoons black pepper
- 2 teaspoons salt
- 2 teaspoons Italian seasoning
- ½ teaspoon onion powder
- ½ teaspoon ground mustard

Directions:
1. Mix all the ingredients together.
2. Rub on your pork.
3. Store in the fridge overnight before cooking ribs.

Nutrition:
Total calories: 69
Protein: 0
Carbs: 17.8
Fat: 0
Fiber: 0

169. Dry Rub for Salmon

Preparation Time: 5 minutes
Cooking Time: 24 hours
Servings: 3 ¼ cups
Ingredients:

- 2 cups brown sugar
- 1 cup kosher salt
- 1 tablespoon black pepper
- 1 tablespoon celery salt
- 1 tablespoon onion powder
- 1 tablespoon garlic powder

Directions:
1. Mix all the ingredients together.
2. To use, rub all over your salmon
3. Cover in plastic wrap then store in the fridge for 24 hours.
4. Rinse before smoking.

Nutrition:
Energy 583 kcal Carbohydrate 149.89 g
Calcium, Ca171 mg
Magnesium, Mg24 mg
Phosphorus, P33 mg
Iron, Fe1.9 mg
Potassium, K322 mg

170. Fruit-Spiced Brine for Pork
Preparation Time: 5 minutes
Cooking Time: 15 minutes
Servings: 2
Ingredients:

- 2 quarts apple juice
- 2 quarts orange juice
- 2 cups salt

- ½ cup brown sugar
- 10 whole cloves
- 1 tablespoon ground nutmeg
- 1 gallon cold water

Directions:
1. Pour apple cider and Orange juice into a big pot.
2. Heat on medium high, adding salt, brown sugar, cloves, and nutmeg.
3. Simmer for 15 minutes, until the sugar and salt have dissolved.
4. Take the pot off the burner and cool for at least 40-60 minutes.
5. Pour in the cold water.
6. To brine, pour over pork and store in the fridge, covered, for 1 hour per pound of meat.
7. Rinse meat before cooking it.

Nutrition:
Energy 277 kcal Carbohydrate67.11 g
Calcium, Ca205 mg Magnesium, Mg33 mg
Phosphorus, P39 mg
Iron, Fe1.79 mg Potassium, K248 mg

171. 6-Ingredient Turkey Brine
Preparation Time: 5 minutes
Cooking Time: 0 minutes
Servings: 12
Ingredients:

- 2 gallons water
- 1 ½ cups canning salt
- 1/3 cup brown sugar
- ¼ cup Worcestershire sauce
- 3 tablespoons minced garlic
- 1 tablespoon black pepper

Directions:
1. Mix all the ingredients in a container big enough for your turkey.
2. Soak turkey in brine, covered, in the fridge for 1-2 days.
3. Rinse meat before smoking.

Nutrition:
Total Fat 0g Saturated Fat 0g
Cholesterol 0mg Sodium 11596mg
Total Carbohydrate 6g Dietary Fiber 0.2g
Total Sugars 4.9g Protein 0.2g

172. Brine for Fish
Preparation Time: 5 minutes

Cooking Time: 0 minutes
Servings: 8 - 10
Ingredients:
- 8 cups water
- 2 cups soy sauce
- 1 ½ cups brown sugar
- ½ cup kosher salt
- 1 ½ tablespoons ground garlic

Directions:
1. Mix all the ingredients together.
2. Pour into a bag with the fish, so it's all covered.
3. Marinate for at least 8 hours.
4. Pat fish dry before smoking.

Nutrition:
Total calories: 110
Protein: 3.2
Carbs: 25.2
Fat: 0
Fiber: 0.4

173. Ranch Mix

Preparation Time: 5 minutes
Cooking Time: 0 minutes
Servings: 16
Ingredients:
- Pepper (two teaspoons)
- Powdered milk (0.5 c.)
- Salt (two teaspoons)
- Paprika (half teaspoon)
- Parsley flakes (1 tbsp., dried-out)
- Onion powder (1 tsp.)
- Onion, dried and minced (2 tbsp.)
- Garlic powder (two teaspoons)

Directions:
1. Mix the ingredients well then store in a dry and cool place for a maximum of 6 months.

Nutrition:
Protein: 1 g

Sugar: 1.2 g
Fiber: 0.3 g
Carbohydrates: 2.5 g
Sodium: 303.9 mg
Cholesterol: 0.4 mg
Total fat: 0.1 g
Total calories: 14

174. Easy, Tasty Blend

Preparation Time: 5 minutes
Cooking Time: 0 minutes
Servings: 84 teaspoons
Ingredients:
- Black pepper, grounded (quarter c.)
- Salt, kosher (1 c.)
- Garlic powder (quarter c.)
- Onion powder (quarter c.)

Directions:
1. Mix all the ingredients very well. You can keep inside any sealed container located in any place that's dry as well as cool for a maximum of 6 months.

Nutrition:
Protein: 0.1g
Fiber: 0.2g
Carbohydrates: 0.8g
Sodium: 1347.9 mg

175. Mopping Sauce, Carolina Style

Preparation Time: 5 minutes
Cooking Time: 0 minutes
Servings: 8
Ingredients:
- Black pepper, ground (0.25 tsp.)
- Salt (0.5 tsp.)
- Mustard, dry (1 tsp.)
- Brown sugar, packed (2 tbsp.)
- Onion powder (one teaspoon)
- Hot sauce (one tablespoon)
- Red pepper flakes (one tablespoon)
- Cider vinegar (one c.)
- Garlic powder (one teaspoon)
- White vinegar, distilled (1 c.)

Directions:

1. Mix your ingredients altogether. Keep them inside an airtight container for a maximum of one month.

Nutrition:
Protein: 0.3g
Sugar: 2.7g
Fiber: 0.4g
Carbohydrates: 3.9g
Sodium: 184.6mg
Monounsaturated Fats: 0.1g
Polyunsaturated Fats: 0.1g
Total fats: 0.2g
Total calories: 28

176. Simple Barbecue Sauce

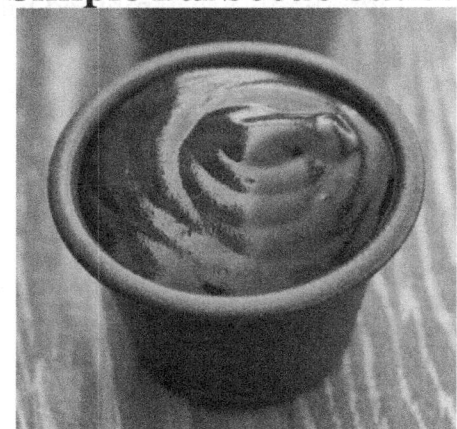

Preparation Time: 5 minutes
Cooking Time: 0 minutes
Servings: 8
Ingredients:

- Cider vinegar (0.25 c.)
- Tomato sauce, organic (15-ounce can)
- Black pepper, ground (half teaspoon)
- Salt (half teaspoon)
- Garlic powder (one tablespoon)
- Hot sauce (one teaspoon)
- Mustard, dry (one tbsp.)
- Onion powder (one tablespoon)
- Paprika, smoked (1 tsp.)
- Paprika, sweet (1 tbsp.)
- Lemon juice, fresh (two tablespoons)

Directions:

1. In a small pan, put the tomato sauce in and then add all the rest of the ingredients. Whisk them all well to coming.
2. Simmer the sauce for 15 minutes until it is thickened.

Nutrition:
Protein: 2.6g
Sugar: 36.2g
Fiber: 3.9g
Carbohydrates: 126.6g
Sodium: 7365mg
Polyunsaturated fats: 0.5g
Monounsaturated fats: 0.1g
Saturated fats: 0.2g
Total fats: 0.9g
Total calories: 116

177. Barbecue Sauce, Jamaican Style

Preparation Time: 5 minutes
Cooking Time: 0 minutes
Servings: 3
Ingredients:

- Allspice (quarter teaspoon)
- Cider vinegar (two tablespoons)
- Nutmeg, ground (quarter teaspoon)
- Cinnamon, ground (quarter teaspoon)
- Salt (one teaspoon)
- Dry mustard, ground (one teaspoon)
- Worcestershire sauce (two tablespoons)
- Sugar, dark brown (2 tbsp.)
- Water (0.5 c.)
- Lime juice (two tablespoons)
- Ketchup (1 c.)
- Scotch Bonnet pepper (1 whole)
- Onion, chopped (0.5 c.)
- Pepper (half teaspoon)
- Olive oil (1 tbsp.)

Directions:

1. Grease your saucepan through the usage of oil with the temperature at med. setting up to the point that it's hot.
2. Then, sauce your pepper as well as your onion until they are soft.

3. Then, add in your remaining raw materials.
4. Heat your mixture to its boiling point, and let it settle down until you get the thickness you want. Take out the pepper and throw it away.
5. Take the sauce off the heat and let it cool.
6. Place the sauce in the refrigerator in a mason jar for a maximum of 2 weeks.

Nutrition:
Protein: 0.2g
Sugar: 16.1g
Fiber: 0.3g
Carbohydrates: 20.6g
Sodium: 872.7mg
Polyunsaturated fats: 0.3g
Monounsaturated fats: 1.7g
Saturated fats: 0.4g
Total fats: 2.4g
Total calories: 103

178. Best Smoker Sauce
Preparation Time: 5 minutes
Cooking Time: 0 minutes
Servings: 32
Ingredients:
- Soy sauce (half cup)
- Ginger, ground (one tablespoon)
- Salt (to taste)
- Your favorite salsa (8 ounces)
- Your favorite BBQ sauce (18-ounce)
- Crushed garlic (one tablespoon)
- Brown sugar, packed (3/4 cup)
- Black pepper, grounded (one tablespoon)

Directions:
1. Mix all the ingredients together. Store in the fried until you're ready to use.

Nutrition:
Protein: 0.4 g
Carbohydrates: 11.5 g
Sodium: 424 mg
Fat: 0.1 g
Total calories: 47

179. Garlic and Honey Sauce
Preparation Time: 10 minutes
Cooking Time: 15 minutes
Servings: 16
Ingredients:
- Water (0.25 c.)
- Ginger root, fresh (1 tsp.)
- Soy sauce (0.25 c.)
- Honey (0.5 c.)
- Brown sugar (0.5 c.)
- Chicken broth (2 c.)
- Garlic cloves (6, crushed)

Directions:
1. Mix all the ingredient together and pour into a pot. Bring it to a boil and let it simmer until all the ingredients are combined for about 5 minutes.

Nutrition:
Protein: 0.5 g
Carbohydrates: 16.8 g
Sodium: 348 mg
Fat: 0.1 g
Total calories: 66

180. Carne Asada Marinade

Preparation Time: 15 minutes
Cooking Time: 2 hours
Servings: 5
Ingredients:
- 1 cloves garlic, chopped
- 1 tsp Lemon juice
- 1/2 cup extra virgin olive oil
- 1/2 tsp Salt
- 1/2 tsp Pepper

Directions:
1. Mix all your ingredients in a bowl.

2. Pour the beef into the bowl and allow to marinate for 2-3hours before grilling.

Nutrition:
Calories: 465kcal
Carbs: 26g
Fat: 15g
Protein: 28g

181. Grapefruit Juice Marinade
Preparation Time: 10 minutes
Cooking Time: 1 hour
Servings: 3
Ingredients:
- 1/2 reduced-sodium soy sauce
- 1 cups grapefruit juice, unsweetened
- 1-1/2 lb. Chicken, bone and skin removed
- 1/4 brown sugar

Directions:
1. Thoroughly mix all your ingredients in a large bowl.
2. Add the chicken and allow it to marinate for 2-3 hours before grilling.

Nutrition:
Calories: 489kcal
Carbs: 21.3
Fat: 12g
Protein: 24g

182. Steak Marinade

Preparation Time: 5 minutes
Cooking Time: 10 minutes
Servings: 2
Ingredients:
- 1 tbsp. Worcestershire sauce
- 1 tbsp. Red wine vinegar
- 1/2 cup barbeque sauce
- 1 tbsp. soy sauce
- 1/4 cup steak sauce
- 1 clove garlic (minced)
- 1 tsp Mustard
- Pepper and salt to taste

Directions:
1. Mix all the ingredients thoroughly.
2. Use immediately or keep refrigerated.

Nutrition:
Calories: 303kcal
Carbs: 42g
Fat: 10g
Protein: 2.4g

CHAPTER 11:

Lamb Recipes

183. Orange Smoked Lamb Leg With Honey Beer Marinade

Preparation Time: 30 minutes
Cooking Time: 2 hours
Servings: 10
Ingredients:
- Boneless lamb leg (4 lbs., 1.8-kg.)

The Marinade
- Beer – 1 ½ cups
- Honey – ½ cup
- Minced garlic – 2 tablespoons
- Onion powder – 1 tablespoon
- Kosher salt – ¼ cup
- Black pepper – 1 tablespoon
- Worcestershire sauce – ¼ cup
- Mustard – 2 tablespoons
- Fresh rosemary – 5 sprigs

The Rub
- Onion powder – 1 tablespoon
- Garlic powder – 1 tablespoon
- Lemon juice – 3 tablespoons
- Apple cider vinegar – 2 tablespoons
- Olive oil – 2 tablespoons
- Kosher salt – 1 tablespoon
- Cumin – 1 teaspoon
- Black pepper – 1 teaspoon
- Cayenne pepper – ½ teaspoon
- Cinnamon – 1 teaspoon
- Nutmeg – 1 teaspoon
- Ground clove – ¼ teaspoon

The Glaze
- Orange marmalade – 1 cup
- Honey – ½ cup

Directions:
1. Pour beer and honey into a container then season with minced garlic, onion powder, kosher salt, black pepper, Worcestershire sauce, mustard, and fresh rosemary. Stir well.
2. Score the boneless lamb leg at several places then add to the beer mixture.
3. Marinate the lamb leg overnight and store in the fridge to keep it fresh.
4. On the next day, remove the lamb leg from the fridge then take it out of the marinade.
5. Combine the rub ingredients—onion powder, garlic powder, lemon juice, apple cider vinegar, olive oil, kosher salt, cumin, black pepper, cayenne pepper, cinnamon, nutmeg, and ground clove then mix well.
6. Rub the marinated lamb leg with the spice mixture then set aside.
7. Next, plug in and turn the Electric Smoker on then set the temperature to 250°F (121°C).
8. Wait until the Electric Smoker has reached the desired temperature then add wood chips to the chip tray.
9. Pour orange juice into the water pan and add ginger to the water pan. Wait until the smoke is ready.
10. Place the seasoned lamb leg on the grill tray inside the Electric Smoker and smoke for 4 hours.
11. In the meantime, mix orange marmalade with honey and stir until incorporated.
12. After 2 hours of smoking, baste the honey orange mixture over the lamb leg once every 30 minutes and continue smoking until the internal

temperature of the smoked lamb leg has reached 145°F (63°C).

13. Remove the smoked lamb leg from the Electric Smoker and let it rest for approximately 10 minutes.
14. Cut the smoked lamb leg into slices and serve.
15. Enjoy.

Nutrition:
Calcium, Ca169 mg
Magnesium, Mg68 mg
Phosphorus, P435 mg
Iron, Fe5.36 mg
Potassium, K866 mg

184. Garlic Mint Smoked Lamb Chops Balsamic

Preparation Time: 10 minutes
Cooking Time: 4 hours
Servings: 10
Ingredients:
- Lamb chops (6-lb., 2.7-kg.)

The Rub
- Dried mint leaves – 1 teaspoon
- Olive oil – ¼ cup
- Minced garlic – ¼ cup
- Black pepper – 1 teaspoon
- Dried rosemary – 1 teaspoon
- Oregano – ½ teaspoon
- Dried thyme – ½ teaspoon
- Kosher salt – 1 ½ tablespoons

The Glaze
- Balsamic vinegar – 1 cup
- Brown sugar – 6 tablespoons

- Black pepper – ½ teaspoon

Directions:
1. Combine the rub ingredients—dried mint leaves, olive oil, minced garlic, black pepper, dried rosemary, oregano, dried thyme, and kosher salt then stir well.
2. Rub the lamb with the spice mixture then set aside.
3. Turn on the Electric Smoker on then set the temperature to 225°F (107°C).
4. Wait until the Electric Smoker has reached the desired temperature then add wood chips to the chip tray. Pour water into the water pan.
5. Put the seasoned lamb chops on the grill tray provided by the Electric Smoker and smoke for 2 hours.
6. Combine balsamic vinegar with brown sugar and black pepper then stir until incorporated.
7. After 2 hours, transfer the lamb chops to a disposable aluminum pan then drizzle the balsamic vinegar mixture over the lamb chops.
8. Continue smoking the lamb chops for another 2 hours or until the internal temperature of the smoked lamb chops has reached 135°F (57°C).
9. Remove the smoked lamb chops from the Electric Smoker then transfer to a serving dish.
10. Serve and enjoy.

Nutrition:
Calcium, Ca58 mg Magnesium, Mg66 mg
Phosphorus, P520 mg Iron, Fe4.35 mg
Potassium, K923 mg Sodium, Na216 mg
Zinc, Zn7.34 mg

185. Sweet Cherry Smoked Lamb Ribs Barbecue

Preparation Time: 10 minutes
Cooking Time: 3 hours
Servings: 10
Ingredients:
- Lamb Ribs (4 lbs., 1.8 kg.)

The Rub

- Brown sugar – ½ cup
- Ginger – 1 tablespoon
- Dried thyme – ½ teaspoon
- Dried tarragon – ½ teaspoon
- Dried marjoram – ½ teaspoon
- Cinnamon – 1 ½ teaspoon
- Black pepper – ½ tablespoon
- Kosher salt – ¾ tablespoon
- Lemon juice – 2 tablespoons

The Glaze

- Cherry cola – 1 cup
- Fresh cherry – 1 cup
- Ketchup – ½ cup
- Onion powder – ½ tablespoon
- Garlic powder – ½ tablespoon
- Worcestershire sauce – ¼ cup
- Lemon juice – 3 tablespoons
- White vinegar – 2 tablespoons
- Soy sauce – 2 tablespoons
- Brown sugar – 3 tablespoons
- Mustard – 1 tablespoon
- Olive oil – 1 ½ tablespoons
- Black pepper – ½ teaspoon
- Liquid smoke – ½ teaspoon

Directions:

1. Cut and trim the excess fat from the lamb ribs then rub with the mixture of brown sugar, ginger, dried thyme, dried marjoram, dried tarragon, cinnamon, black pepper, kosher salt, and lemon juice. Set aside.
2. Plug in and turn the Electric Smoker on then set the temperature to 225°F (107°C).
3. Wait until the Electric Smoker has reached the desired temperature then add wood chips to the chip tray. Pour water into the water pan.
4. Once the Electric Smoker is ready, place the seasoned lamb ribs on the grill tray inside the Electric Smoker and smoke for an hour.
5. In the meantime, place the entire glaze ingredients—fresh cherries, cherry cola, ketchup, garlic powder, onion powder, Worcestershire sauce, lemon juice, white vinegar, soy sauce, brown sugar, mustard, olive oil, black pepper, and liquid smoke in a blender then blend until smooth.
6. After an hour of smoking, baste the glaze mixture over the lamb ribs then wrap with aluminum foil.
7. Return the wrapped lamb ribs to the Electric Smoker and smoke for about 2 hours or until the internal temperature has reached 63°C
8. Once it is done, remove the smoked lamb ribs from the Electric Smoker and unwrap it.
9. Transfer the smoked lamb ribs to a serving dish and enjoy!

Nutrition:
Calcium, Ca18 mg
Magnesium, Mg8 mg
Phosphorus, P22 mg
Iron, Fe0.89 mg
Potassium, K152 mg
Sodium, Na256 mg
Zinc, Zn0.14 mg

186. Minty Apple Smoked Pulled Lamb Barbecue

Preparation Time: 30 minutes
Cooking Time: 5 hours 30 minutes
Servings: 10
Ingredients:

- Boneless lamb shoulder (4 lbs., 1.8 kg.)
- The rub
- brown sugar – ½ cup
- kosher salt – 1 tablespoon
- black pepper – 1 teaspoon
- dried thyme – 1 teaspoon
- smoked paprika – 1 ½ teaspoons
- The spray
- Apple juice – 1 ½ cups
- Apple cider vinegar – 3 tablespoons
- Fresh mint leaves – 3 sprigs
- The Sauce
- Apple juice – 1 cup
- Apple cider vinegar – 1 tablespoon
- Olive oil – 3 tablespoons
- Onion powder – 1 teaspoon
- Garlic powder – 1 teaspoon

- Brown sugar – 3 tablespoons
- Mint sauce – ¼ cup

Directions:

1. Pour the spray ingredients—apple juice and apple cider vinegar into a spray bottle then add fresh mint leaves. Shake until combined then set aside.
2. Score the lamb shoulder at several places then rub with brown sugar, kosher salt, black pepper, dried thyme, and smoked paprika. Set aside.
3. Plug in and turn the Electric Smoker on then set the temperature to 225°F (107°C).
4. Wait until the Electric Smoker has reached the desired temperature then add wood chips to the chip tray. Pour apple juice into the water pan.
5. Place the seasoned lamb shoulder on the grill tray provided by the Electric Smoker then smoke for approximately 5 hours. Spray the apple juice mixture over the lamb shoulder once every 30 minutes.
6. In the meantime, place the entire sauce ingredients—apple juice, apple cider vinegar, olive oil, garlic powder, brown sugar, and mint sauce in a bowl then stir until incorporated.
7. Once the internal temperature of the smoked lamb has reached 165°F (74°C) baste half of the sauce over it and wrap with aluminum foil.
8. Return the lamb shoulder to the Electric Smoker and smoke for about 30 minutes.
9. Remove the smoked lamb shoulder from the Electric Smoker then unwrap it. Using a fork or a sharp knife shred the smoked lamb shoulder into pieces.
10. Transfer the smoked lamb to a serving dish then drizzle the remaining sauce on top. Mix well.
11. Serve and enjoy.

Nutrition:
Calcium, Ca19 mg
Magnesium, Mg43 mg
Phosphorus, P327 mg
Iron, Fe2.28 mg
Potassium, K688 mg
Sodium, Na167 mg
Zinc, Zn6.94 mg

187. Spicy Brown Smoked Lamb Ribs

Preparation Time: 30 minutes
Cooking Time: 4 hours
Servings: 10
Ingredients:

- Lamb ribs (3,5 lb., 1.6 kg.)
- The Rub
- Brown sugar – ¼ cup
- Kosher salt – 1 tablespoon
- Pepper – 1 teaspoon
- The Sauce
- Apricot jam – 2 cups
- Dried chilies – 2 tablespoons
- Diced onion – 2 tablespoons
- Minced garlic – 1 tablespoon
- Ground cloves – ¼ teaspoon
- Black peppercorns – ½ teaspoon
- Ground coriander – ½ teaspoon
- Cumin – ¾ teaspoon
- Oregano – 1 teaspoon
- Kosher salt – ½ teaspoon
- Canola oil – 3 tablespoons
- Ground cinnamon – 1 teaspoon

Directions:

1. Pour water over the dried chilies then soak for approximately 10 minutes or until softened. Discard the water.
2. Place the softened chilies in a blender then add apricot jam, diced onion, ground cloves, minced garlic, black peppercorns, ground coriander, cumin, oregano, kosher salt, canola oil, and ground cinnamon. Blend until smooth then set aside.
3. Plug in and turn the Electric Smoker on then set the temperature to 225°F (107°C).

4. Wait until the Electric Smoker has reached the desired temperature then add wood chips to the chip tray. Pour apple juice into the water pan.
5. Rub the lamb ribs with brown sugar, kosher salt, and pepper then place in the Electric Smoker. Smoked the lamb ribs for an hour.
6. After an hour of smoking, take the lamb ribs out of the Electric Smoker and baste apricot sauce over it.
7. Wrap the glazed lamb ribs with aluminum foil then continue smoking for 3 hours or until the internal temperature has reached 63C
8. Once it is done, remove the smoked lamb ribs from the Electric Smoker and let it rest for approximately 30 minutes.
9. Unwrap the smoked lamb ribs then transfer to a serving dish.
10. Serve and enjoy.

Nutrition:
Calcium, Ca48 mg
Magnesium, Mg52 mg
Phosphorus, P338 mg
Iron, Fe3.81 mg
Potassium, K573 mg
Sodium, Na319 mg
Zinc, Zn7.03 mg

188. Chinese Style Lamb Shanks

Preparation Time: 15 minutes
Cooking Time: 10 hours
Servings: 2
Ingredients:
- 2 (1¼lb) lamb shanks
- 1-2 cups water
- ½ cup brown sugar
- ½ cup rice wine
- ½ cup soy sauce
- 3 tbsp dark sesame oil
- 4 (1½x½-inch) orange zest strips
- 2 (3-inch long) cinnamon sticks
- 1½ tsp Chinese five spice powder

Directions:
1. Soak apple wood chips in water for at least 1 hour.
2. Heat the smoker to 225-250 degrees F. Load soaked apple wood chips.
3. With a sharp knife, pierce each lamb shank at many places.
4. In a bowl, add remaining all ingredients and mix until sugar is dissolved.
5. In a large roasting pan, place lamb shanks and top with sugar mixture evenly.
6. In a foil pan, transfer the lamb shanks with sugar mixture.
7. Place the foil pan into the smoker and cook for about 8-10 hours, flipping after every 30 minutes. (If required, add enough water to keep the liquid ½-inch over.)
8. Serve hot.

Nutrition:
Calories: 1500
Carbohydrates: 68g
Protein: 163.3g
Fat: 62g
Sugar: 52.3g
Sodium: 4000mg
Fiber: 0.5g

189. Cola Flavored Lamb Ribs
Preparation Time: 15 minutes
Cooking Time: 3 hours
Servings: 8
Ingredients:
- 4 (1-1½lb) lamb rib racks, trimmed
- 1 tbsp unsweetened cocoa powder
- 1 tbsp brown sugar
- 1 tbsp smoked paprika
- 1 tbsp salt
- 1 tbsp cracked black pepper
- 1 cup cherry cola

Directions:

1. Heat the smoker to 225 degreesF.
2. With a sharp knife, make ½ x ¼-inch cuts in each rib rack.
3. In a bowl, add remaining ingredients except cherry cola and mix well.
4. Generously rub the rib racks with sugar mixture.
5. In a spray bottle, place the cherry cola.
6. Arrange the rib racks into the smoker and cook for about 2½-3 hours, coating with cherry cola after every 1 hour.

Nutrition:
Calories: 547
Carbohydrates: 2.5g
Protein: 64.3g
Fat: 29.5g
Sugar: 1.2g
Sodium: 1060mg
Fiber: 0.8g

190. Glorious Lamb Shoulder
Preparation Time: 15 minutes
Cooking Time: 7 hours
Servings: 10
Ingredients:

- 1 (7lb) boneless lamb shoulder, excess fat trimmed
- 1½ tbsp ancho chili powder
- ½ tbsp dried oregano
- ½ tbsp dry mustard powder
- ½ tbsp ground allspice
- ½ tbsp ground coriander
- ½ tbsp garlic powder
- ½ tbsp celery salt
- ½ tbsp smoked sweet paprika
- 2 tbsp canola oil
- 1-2 cups BBQ sauce
- Salt and freshly ground black pepper

Directions:

1. Add all the ingredients except the lamb, canola oil and BBQ sauce and mix well.
2. Rub the lamb shoulder with the spice mixture generously.
3. Roll the meat and with kitchen string, tie at 1-inch intervals.
4. Cover the lamb shoulder and refrigerate overnight.
5. Remove the lamb shoulder from refrigerator and coat with oil evenly.
6. Set aside in room temperature for about 30 minutes before cooking.
7. Heat the smoker to 225 degrees F. Load cherry wood chips.
8. Place the lamb shoulder into the smoker, fat side up and cook for about 6-7 hours.
9. In the last 30 minutes, coat the shoulder with some of the BBQ sauce.
10. Transfer the lamb shoulder onto a cutting board and discard the kitchen twine.
11. Set aside for about 20 minutes before serving.
12. With a sharp knife, cut the leg of lamb in desired sized slices and serve.

Nutrition:
Calories: 699
Carbohydrates: 19.7g
Protein: 89.6g
Fat: 26.6g
Sugar: 13.3g
Sodium: 830mg
Fiber: 1g

191. Divine Lamb Chops
Preparation Time: 15 minutes
Cooking Time: 33 hours
Servings: 4
Ingredients:

- 4 (10-ounce) lamb shoulder chops
- 4 cups buttermilk
- 1 cup cold water
- ¼ cup kosher salt
- 2 tbsp olive oil, as required
- 2 tbsp Texas style rub

Directions:

1. In a large bowl, add buttermilk, water and salt and stir until salt is dissolved.

2. Add chops and coat with mixture evenly.
3. Refrigerate for at least 4 hours.
4. Remove the chops from bowl and rinse under cold water.
5. Coat the chops with olive oil and then sprinkle with rub evenly.
6. Heat the smoker to 240 degrees F.
7. Arrange the chops on smoker and cook for about 25-30 minute or until desired doneness.
8. Meanwhile Heat the broiler.
9. Broil the chops for about 2-3 minutes or until browned.

Nutrition:
Calorie: 585
Carbohydrates: 11.7g
Protein: 63.3g
Fat: 31.7g
Sugar: 11.7g
Sodium: 7500mg
Fiber: 0g

192. Foolproof Leg of Lamb

Preparation Time: 15 minutes
Cooking Time: 2 hours 30 minutes
Servings: 8
Ingredients:
For Leg of Lamb:
- 1 (4-5lb) leg of lamb, butterflied
- 2-3 tbsp olive oil

For Filling:
- 1 (8-ounce) package cream cheese, softened
- ¼ cup cooked bacon, crumbled
- 1 jalapeño pepper, seeded and chopped

For Spice Mixture:
- 1 tbsp dried rosemary, crushed
- 2 tsp garlic powder
- 1 tsp onion powder
- 1 tsp paprika
- 1 tsp cayenne pepper
- Salt, to taste

Directions:
1. For filling: in a bowl, add all ingredients and mix until well combined.

2. For spice mixture: in another small bowl, mix together all ingredients.
3. Place the leg of lamb onto a smooth surface.
4. Sprinkle the inside of leg with some spice mixture.
5. Place filling mixture over the inside surface evenly and roll tightly.
6. With a butcher's twine, tie the roll to secure the filling.
7. Coat the outer side of roll with olive oil evenly and then sprinkle with spice mixture.
8. Heat the smoker to 225-240 degrees F. Load cherry wood chips.
9. Arrange the leg of lamb into the smoker and cook for about 2-2½ hours.
10. Place the leg of lamb onto a cutting board and loosely cover with a piece of foil for about 20-25 minutes before serving.
11. With a sharp knife, cut the leg of lamb in desired sized slices and serve.

Nutrition:
Calories: 758 Carbohydrates: 2.1g
Protein: 86g Fat: 43.1g
Sugar: 0.5g Sodium: 640mg
Fiber: 0.5g

193. Crowd Pleasing Meatloaf

Preparation Time: 20 minutes
Cooking Time: 4 hours
Servings: 6
Ingredients:
For Meatloaf:
- 2 lbs ground beef

- ½ cup panko bread crumbs
- 2 eggs, lightly beaten
- ¼ cup milk
- ½ medium red onion, grated
- 2 garlic cloves, minced
- 2 tbsp whiskey
- 1 tbsp Worcestershire sauce
- 1 tbsp steak rub
- 6-ounce pepper jack cheese, cut into strips

For Sauce:

- ½ cup ketchup
- 1/3 cup brown sugar
- ¼ cup whiskey
- 1 tbsp steak rub
- 2 tsp red pepper flakes, crushed

Directions:

1. Heat the smoker to 225 degrees F.
2. Soak oak wood chips in water for at least 1 hour.
3. For meatloaf: in a large bowl, add all ingredients and mix until well combined.
4. Place half of meat mixture in the bottom of a grill basket.
5. Place the cheese over meatloaf, leaving about 1-inch on all sides.
6. Move the remaining meat mixture on top and press the edges together to seal completely.
7. For sauce: in a small bowl, add all the ingredients and mix until well combined.
8. Spread the sauce on top of meatloaf evenly.
9. Place the meatloaf into the smoker and cook, covered for about 4 hours.
10. Transfer the meatloaf onto a wire rack for about 5 minutes before slicing.
11. Cut into desired sized slices and serve.

Nutrition:
Calories: 552 Carbohydrates: 22.6g
Protein: 56.9g Fat: 20.9g Sugar: 14.5g
Sodium: 727mg
Fiber: 0.9g

194. 2 Meats Combo Meatloaf
Preparation Time: 20 minutes
Cooking Time: 4 hours
Servings: 6
Ingredients:

- 1½ lbs ground pork
- 1½ cups BBQ sauce, divided
- 2 lbs ground beef chuck
- 2 roasted bell peppers, chopped
- 1/3 cup onion, chopped finely
- 4 garlic cloves, minced
- 2 eggs, beaten
- ¾ cup fresh breadcrumbs
- 1 tbsp dried oregano, crushed
- Salt and freshly ground black pepper

Directions:

1. Heat the smoker to 225 degrees F.
2. In a large bowl, add ½ cup of BBQ sauce and remaining all ingredients and mix until well combined.
3. Arrange a 24-inch piece of foil in a small baking sheet, doubling it over by folding it half.
4. Mold the sides of foil upwards to make a loaf pan.
5. Place the meat mixture in loaf pan and press to form a meatloaf
6. Place the loaf pan over smoker rack and cook for about 3-4 hours.
7. In the last hour of coking, coat the meatloaf with the remaining BBQ sauce.
8. Transfer the meatloaf onto a wire rack for about 5 minutes before slicing.
9. Cut into desired sized slices and serve.

Nutrition:
Calories: 736
Carbohydrates: 36.8g
Protein: 59.4g
Fat: 37.2g
Sugar: 19.5g
Sodium: 1012mg
Fiber: 1.7g

195. Rosemary-Smoked Lamb Chops
Preparation Time: 15 minutes
Cooking Time: 2 hours and 5 minutes
Servings: 4
Ingredients:
- 4½ pounds bone-in lamb chops
- 2 tablespoons olive oil
- Salt
- Freshly ground black pepper
- 1 bunch fresh rosemary

Directions:
1. Heat the smoker to 180°F.
2. Rub the lamb generously with olive oil and season on both sides with salt and pepper.
3. Spread the rosemary directly on the grill grate, creating a surface area large enough for all the chops to rest on. Place the chops on the rosemary and smoke until they reach an internal temperature of 135°F.
4. Increase the smoker's temperature to 450°F, remove the rosemary, and continue to cook the chops until their internal temperature reaches 145°F.
5. Take off the lamb from the grill and let them rest for 5 minutes before serving.

Nutrition:
Calcium, Ca57 mg
Magnesium, Mg123 mg
Phosphorus, P1011 mg
Iron, Fe8.43 mg
Potassium, K1789 mg
Sodium, Na327 mg
Zinc, Zn16.14 mg

196. Classic Lamb Chops
Preparation Time: 10 minutes
Cooking Time: 30 minutes
Servings: 4
Ingredients:
- Wood Flavor: Alder
- 4 (8-ounce) bone-in lamb chops
- 2 tablespoons olive oil
- 1 batch Rosemary-Garlic Lamb Seasoning

Directions:
1. Supply your smoker with wood chips and follow the manufacturer's specific start-up procedure. Heat the grill to 350°F. Close the lid
2. Rub the lamb generously with olive oil and coat them on both sides with the seasoning.
3. Place the chops on the grill grate and grill until their internal temperature reaches 145°F. Remove the lamb from the grill and serve immediately.

Nutrition:
Calcium, Ca7 mg Magnesium, Mg14 mg
Phosphorus, P112 mg Iron, Fe0.98 mg
Potassium, K200 mg
Sodium, Na36 mg Zinc, Zn1.79 mg

197. Seared lamb chops
Preparation Time: 10 minutes
Cooking Time: 20 minutes
Servings: 4
Ingredients:
- 4 (8-ounce) bone-in lamb chops
- 2 tablespoons olive oil
- 1 batch Rosemary-Garlic Lamb Seasoning

Directions:
1. Heat the smoker to 500F. Close the lid
2. Rub the lamb chops with olive oil and coat them on both sides with the seasoning.
3. Put the chops on the grill grate and grill until they reach an internal temperature of 120°F for rare, 130°F for medium, and 145F for well-done. Remove the lamb from the grill then serve immediately.

Nutrition:
Calcium, Ca7 mg Magnesium, Mg14 mg
Phosphorus, P112 mg
Iron, Fe0.98 mg Potassium, K200 mg
Sodium, Na36 mg
Zinc, Zn1.79 mg

198. Roasted Leg Of Lamb

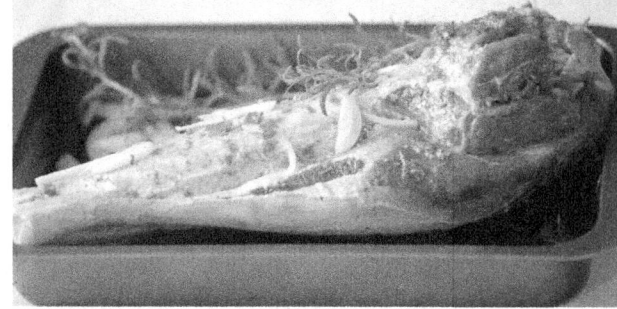

Preparation Time: 15 minutes
Cooking Time: 1-2 hours
Servings: 4
Ingredients:

- 1 (6- to 8-pound) boneless leg of lamb
- 2 batches Rosemary-Garlic Lamb Seasoning

Directions:

1. Heat the smoker to 350°F. Close the lid
2. Using your hands, rub the lamb leg with the seasoning, rubbing it under and around any netting.
3. Put the lamb directly on the grill grate and smoke until its internal temperature reaches 145°F.
4. Take off the lamb from the grill and let it rest for 20 to 30 minutes, before removing the netting, slicing, and serving.

Nutrition:
Calcium, Ca92 mg
Magnesium, Mg209 mg
Phosphorus, P1769 mg
Iron, Fe15.91 mg
Potassium, K2979 m
Sodium, Na726 mg
Zinc, Zn31.76 mg

199. Hickory-Smoked Leg Of Lamb

Preparation Time: 15 minutes
Cooking Time: 5-7 hours
Servings: 4
Ingredients:

- 1 (6- to 8-pound) boneless leg of lamb
- 2 batches Rosemary-Garlic Lamb Seasoning

Directions:

1. Heat the smoker to 225F. Close the lid
2. Using your hands, rub the lamb leg with the seasoning, rubbing it under and around any netting.
3. Move the lamb directly on the grill grate and smoke until its internal temperature reaches 145F.
4. Take off the lamb from the grill and let it rest for 20 to 30 minutes, before removing the netting, slicing, and serving.

Nutrition:
Calcium, Ca92 mg Magnesium, Mg209 mg
Phosphorus, P1769 mg
Iron, Fe15.91 mg Potassium, K2979 m
Sodium, Na726 mg
Zinc, Zn31.76 mg

200. Smoked Rack Of Lamb

Preparation Time: 25 minutes
Cooking Time: 4-6 hours
Servings: 4
Ingredients:

- 1 (2-pound) rack of lamb
- 1 batch Rosemary-Garlic Lamb Seasoning

Directions:

1. Heat the smoker to 225°F. Close the lid
2. Using a boning knife, score the bottom fat portion of the rib meat.
3. Using your hands, rub the rack of lamb all over with the seasoning, making sure it penetrates into the scored fat.
4. Place the rack directly on the grill grate, fat-side up, and smoke until its internal temperature reaches 145°F.
5. Take off the rack from the grill and let it rest for 20 to 30 minutes, before slicing it into individual ribs to serve.

Nutrition:
Calcium, Ca92 mg Magnesium, Mg209 mg
Phosphorus, P1769 mg Iron, Fe15.91 mg
Potassium, K2979 m Sodium, Na726 mg
Zinc, Zn31.76 mg

201. Roast Rack Of Lamb

Preparation Time: 10 minutes
Cooking Time: 1 hour
Servings: 6-8
Ingredients:

- 1 (2-pound) rack of lamb
- 1 batch Rosemary-Garlic Lamb Seasoning

Directions:

1. Heat the smoker to 450°F.
2. Using a boning knife, score the bottom fat portion of the rib meat.
3. Using your hands, rub the rack of lamb with the lamb seasoning, making sure it penetrates into the scored fat.
4. Place the rack directly on the grill grate and smoke until its internal temperature reaches 145F.
5. Take off the rack from the grill and let it rest for 20 to 30 minutes, before slicing into individual ribs to serve.

Nutrition:
Calcium, Ca92 mg
Magnesium, Mg209 mg
Phosphorus, P1769 mg
Iron, Fe15.91 mg
Potassium, K2979 m
Sodium, Na726 mg
Zinc, Zn31.76 mg

CHAPTER 12:

Cold smoke and game recipes

202. Cold smoked salmon

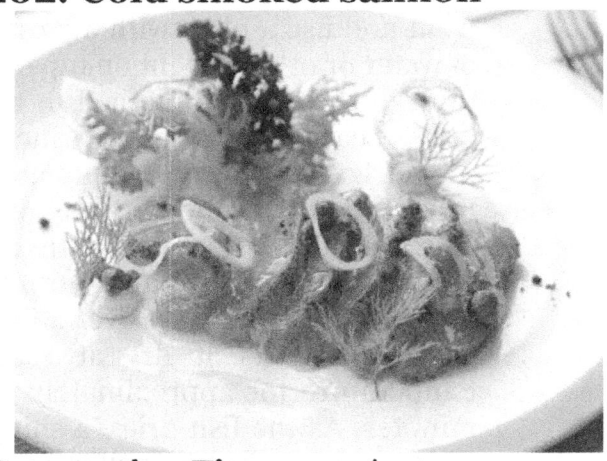

Preparation Time: 30 minutes
Cooking Time: 2 hours
Servings: 4
Ingredients:

- 2 – 3 pounds salmon fillet fresh
- cold water
- 2 tablespoons crushed black pepper
- 3 cups brown sugar
- 3 cups Kosher salt or sea salt or enough to cover you salmon
- 4 cloves of crushed garlic
- 1 tsp crushed fennel seeds

Directions:

1. Place the salmon fillet on a flat surface flesh side up. If the salmon is not at room temperature, let sit for an hour or so for it to come to room temperature. Run your fingers overtop of the skin side of the salmon fillet and feel for the ends of any pin bones. Pull out any pin bones with a pair of tweezers by pulling the ends of the pin bones. Once all the pin bones have been removed, run your fingers over one more time to double check all pin bones have been removed. Clean the salmon fillet and make sure there is no muck on them

2. In a mixing bowl mix together the Kosher salt (or sea salt), black pepper, brown sugar crushed fennel seeds and garlic.

3. Place the salmon in a glass baking dish flesh side up. Ensure you place the salmon inside the dish so it has plenty of room and no filets are touching. Spread out 1/3 of the cure. Place the salmon fillets on top of the cure making sure that the cure extends around ½ inch from each side of the salmon. Spread the remaining cure on the top side of the salmon, coating each salmon fillet completely with no gaps or holes.

4. Cover the dish completely with plastic wrap and place the salmon in the coolest part of your refrigerator for 24 – 48 hours to cure. For best results place a weight on top of your salmon while in the cure. I recommend something like a pie dish or a baking tray with a couple of cans of food. You are looking for around 1 – 1.5 pounds of weight to help draw out moisture. The key with the cure is the longer, the better.

5. Place the salmon In a large bowl filled with 3 inches of cold water soak the fillets for 30 minutes. After 30 minutes drain well with lots of fresh cold water to remove any salt and muck.

6. Pat the salmon dry on both sides with paper towels then place the salmon skin side down, uncovered

on a wire rack on top of a sheet pan to air dry. Place in the refrigerator and let air dry for around 4 hours. The fillets should feel a little sticky at this point. This is when the pellicle forms. Don't worry the salmon fillets will not stick to the wire rack.

7. Prepare your smoker for cold smoking as per your manufacturer's instructions. Remember cold smoking temperatures are important so ensure your temperatures never exceed 86 degrees Fahrenheit.

8. Place the salmon in your smoker flesh side up. Let the salmon go through the smoking process until it feels leathery, firm and has a nice bronze color. This should take a minimum of 12 hours right up to 20 hours.

9. Before serving wrap the salmon in butcher/baking paper and rest in the refrigerator for a minimum of 4 hours. Ideally leave overnight.

10. Diagonally cut thin (or thick depending on your preference) slices with a very sharp knife and garnish with lots of fresh dill, lemon slices, black pepper, capers, red onion, crusty bread and a squeeze of lemon juice. If you are feeling fancy a garnish of teaspoon of lemon zest will also

Nutrition:
Energy 607 kcal Calcium, Ca37 mg
Magnesium, Mg36 mg Phosphorus, P214 mg
Iron, Fe3.45 mg Potassium, K477 mg
Sodium, Na1543 mg Zinc, Zn6.19 mg

203. Cold smoked trout
Preparation Time: 45 minutes
Cooking Time: 2 hours
Servings: 7
Ingredients:
- 2 1/2 to 1-inch thick trout fillets (or halves, or a whole fish, cleaned)
- 2 quarts water
- 1/2 cup kosher salt
- 1/4 cup sugar
- 1/2 teaspoon pink curing salt #1 (optional)
- 2 bay leaves (crumbled or torn)
- 1 whole clove
- 4 whole allspice
- 1/2 teaspoon dried sage

Directions:
1. Stir the brine ingredients until the salt and sugar dissolve. Add the trout and use a plate with a jar full of water or other weight on top of it to keep the fish submerged in the brine. Leave the fish in the brine in the refrigerator for 12 to 24 hours.

2. Rinse the trout under cold water and then pat it dry with either a clean dishtowel or paper towels. Lay it out on a rack set over a dish or tray and let it dry at room temperature for approximately 30 minutes. As the fish dries, a shiny, tacky layer called a pellicle will form. The pellicle seals in juices that keep the fish tender and also gives the smoke something to adhere to. This gives the final product a richer smoke flavor than it would have otherwise.

3. While the fish is brining and drying, get your smoker and smoking components ready. If you are using soaked wood chips, begin soaking them. Only use hardwoods such as pear, apple, and birch for the wood chips.

4. Cold smoke the trout for two to three hours at between 90 and 100 F. On the hottest days of summer, the ambient air temperature may be higher than this, but smoking trout is a cool weather project. Add the soaked hardwood chips as needed to keep a consistent amount of smoke wafting over the fish. Open the vents or add water to the bowl in some smoker models (as needed) to maintain the temperature.

5. Separately from the smoker, start another wood fire or get some charcoal burning. A charcoal chimney is useful for this. In the smoker bring the temperature up to 225 F. Insert a digital thermometer into the thickest part of the fish. Maintain the 225 F temperature as closely as you can until the internal temperature of the fish reaches 180 F. This will usually take about three to four hours, but if you've got an especially big fish and are smoking it whole, it could take as long as 10 hours. During this time, continue to add soaked hardwood chips to keep the smoke surrounding the fish.

6. Once the internal temperature of the fish reaches 180 F, maintain it for an additional 30 minutes before removing the trout from the smoker.

7. Once the trout has completely cooled to at least room temperature (or colder if you're undertaking this project outdoors on a chilly day), wrap it tightly in foil, butcher's paper or vacuum seal it. Trout smoked by this method will keep in the refrigerator for up to one month and in the freezer, for at least three months.

Nutrition:
Calories: 736
Carbohydrates: 36.8g
Protein: 59.4g
Fat: 37.2g
Sugar: 19.5g
Sodium: 1012mg
Fiber: 1.7g

204. Cold Smoked Bacon
Preparation Time: 25 minutes
Cooking Time: 20 minutes
Servings: 4
Ingredients:
- "raw" side bacon
- pork belly

Directions:
1. Block the main flue with a wet towel
2. Open the butterfly to the warmer
3. Maintain warmer at 110

Nutrition:
Calories: 25 Cal
Carbs: 0 g
Fat: 2 g
Protein: 4 g
Fiber: 0 g.

205. Smoked Venison Tenderloin (marinated)

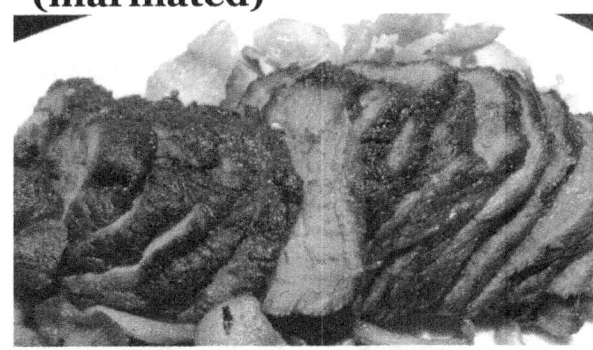

Preparation Time: 7-14 hours
Cooking Time: 2 hours
Servings: 4
Ingredients:
- 2 venison tenderloins, 6 to 8 ounces each
- 1/3 cup drinkable dry red wine
- 1/4 cup extra virgin olive oil (EVOO)
- 1 TBS soy sauce or tamari
- 1 tsp brown or Dijon mustard
- 1 tsp honey or maple syrup
- 1/2 small onion, diced
- 2 cloves garlic, minced
- 1 tsp dried rosemary
- 1 tsp sea salt
- 1 tsp cracked black pepper

Directions:
1. Trim any silver skin off of the tenderloins. Prepare the marinade in a bowl, whisking together the 10 last ingredients on the list. Place the tenderloins in a large, sealable baggie or 2. Stand the bags up in a baking dish. Pour the marinade over the venison. Squeeze any air out, seal the bags, and massage

lightly to coat the meat. Place the dish with the bag or bags in the refrigerator for up to 12 hours, but not less than 4.

2. Take the venison out of the refrigerator 20 minutes before you start your smoker. Remove a grill rack from your smoker and place on paper towels (to catch marinade drippings). Prepare the smoker by adding wood chips to the tray and water to the bowl. Preheat the smoker to 250°F. Open the top vent.

3. When the smoker is up to temperature, remove the venison from the marinade and place on the rack. Discard extra marinade. Put the rack in the smoker and cook for approximately 2 hours, checking the internal temperature at 60 minutes. You want the meat to be between 140°F and 150°F, depending on how rare or well done you like it. Replenish the wood chips and water every 45 to 60 minutes.

4. Remove the venison to a cutting board and tent with foil. Allow it to rest for approximately 20 minutes. Slice thinly and serve with some autumn sides.

Nutrition:

Calories: 300 Sugar: 2 g
Sodium: 646 mg
Fat: 17 g
Saturated Fat: 3 g
Unsaturated Fat: 11 g
Trans Fat: 0 g
Carbohydrates: 3 g
Fiber: 0 g
Protein: 33 g
Cholesterol: 75 mg

206. Wild game cottage pie

Preparation Time: 20 minutes
Cooking Time: 1 hours 30 min
Servings: 4
Ingredients:

- 1 lb ground bison
- 1/2 lb elk steak, minced / thinly sliced
- 2 tbsp unsalted butter
- 3 tbsp olive oil, extra virgin
- 8 oz mushrooms, sliced
- 1 white onion, finely chopped
- 1 shallot, finely chopped
- 2 cloves garlic, minced
- 1 cup zucchini, finely chopped
- 2 tbsp flour
- 2 tbsp tomato paste
- 1 1/2 cups beef broth
- 1 cup red wine, cabernet or merlot
- 1 tsp sea salt
- 1 tsp granulated garlic powder
- 1 bay leaf

CAULIFLOWER TOPPING

- 1 head cauliflower, trimmed, florets coarsely chopped
- 4 tbsp unsalted butter
- 1 tsp sea salt
- 1/2 cup parmesan cheese, grated
- 1 tsp dried parsley
- 2 green onions, finely chopped

Directions:

1. Heat a skillet over medium heat and add 1 tablespoon of olive oil. Carefully add the cubed meat to the skillet frying until lightly browned on the edges. Add the ground game and continue cooking until done. Remove from heat.

2. Heat a large saucepan over medium heat and add butter and 2 tablespoons of olive oil. Toss in the mushrooms, onions, shallots, zucchini and garlic cooking until the onions soften about 15 minutes.

3. Sprinkle flour over the vegetables and stir to coat. Whisk in the beef broth, tomato paste and red wine and cook for a few minutes. Add the browned game meat to the saucepan and season with salt and garlic powder. Add a bay leaf and reduce the heat simmering for 45 minutes or until the gravy thickens.

4. Cook cauliflower florets in a large saucepan of boiling water for 15

minutes or until tender. Remove from pan and drain. Add the cauliflower back into the pan and puree with an immersion blender or potato masher. Add butter and season with salt. Cover with a lid to keep cauliflower mash warm.

5. Pre-heat the smoker to 400 degrees.

6. Pour the meat into an oven proof dish or pie pan and top with the cauliflower mash. Season the mash with Parmesan cheese and dried parsley flakes (I also like to drizzle a little extra virgin olive oil on top). Bake for 25-30 minutes or until the topping is golden browned.

7. Garnish with chopped green onions and serve immediately.

Nutrition:
Calories: 552
Carbohydrates: 22.6g
Protein: 56.9g
Fat: 20.9g
Sugar: 14.5g
Sodium: 727mg
Fiber: 0.9g

207. Wild Game Jerky marinade
Preparation Time: 2 days
Cooking Time: 4 hours
Servings: 4
Ingredients:
- 3 lbs elk or venison
- 1/2 cup brown sugar
- 1/4 cup soy sauce
- 1/4 cup Worcestershire sauce
- 1/4 cup balsamic vinegar
- 1 tbsp granulated garlic powder
- 1 tbsp granulated onion powder
- 6-8 smoked serrano chile peppers, crushed

Directions:
1. Semi-defrost the elk or venison meat to allow for easier slicing. Using a sharp blade, carefully slice the strips of game meat to be roughly ¼ inch thick.

2. In a non-reactive bowl, combine remaining ingredients mixing well.

Add the sliced meat to the marinade and stir to combine. Cover the bowl with plastic wrap or put in a Ziploc storage bag and seal. Refrigerate for 48 hours.

3. Drain the meat in a colander to remove excess marinade. Lay jerky slices on stackable trays allowing ½ inch of spacing between each one. Set the dehydrator temperature to 140 degrees Fahrenheit and dry for 3-4 hours. Check the jerky after two hours and rotate trays. Checking the jerky allows you to remove smaller pieces of jerky that will dry faster. Remove the jerky when done and store in an airtight container or paper bag.

Nutrition:
Calories: 312
Total fat: 9g
Net carbs: 1g
Protein: 55g

208. Meatballs with Candied Carrots
Preparation Time: 1 hour
Cooking Time: 50 minutes
Servings: 2
Ingredients:
- 1 pound ground game meat
- 1 medium onion, grated (cheese grater)
- 1 garlic clove, finely chopped
- 1 teaspoon coriander
- 1 teaspoon cumin
- 1/2 teaspoon turmeric
- 1/2 teaspoon garam masala
- 1/2 teaspoon sea salt

Curry Candied Carrots
- 2 cups carrots, shaved into strips (potato peeler)
- 2 tablespoons unsalted butter
- 1 shallot, finely chopped
- 2 cloves garlic, finely chopped
- 1 tablespoon dark brown sugar
- 1/2 teaspoon garam masala
- 1/4 teaspoon sea salt

Directions:

1. Preheat smoker to 375° F.
2. Add all meatball ingredients to a bowl and mix everything together. Using your hands, shape 6 large meatballs and place on a non-stick baking sheet. Bake for 30 minutes or until done.
3. While the meatballs are baking, heat a skillet over low heat and melt the butter. Add the chopped shallots and garlic. When the garlic is fragrant, add the shaved carrots to the skillet. Season the carrots with brown sugar, garam masala and sea salt. Slow cook the carrots until they become soft and golden brown around the edges. Remove from heat when done.
4. Serve the curried game meatballs and cooked carrots with a side of brown or white steamed rice

Nutrition:

Calories 212,5
Carbohydrate Content 27,5 g
Cholesterol Content 30 mg
Fat Content 5 g
Fiber Content 5 g
Protein Content 16,5 g
Saturated Fat Content 1 g
Sodium Content 179,5 mg
Sugar Content 2,5 g
Monounsaturated Fat Content 2,5 g
Polyunsaturated Fat Content 0,75 g

CHAPTER 13:

Turkey Recipes

209. Smoked Turkey

Preparation Time: 1 hour 30 minutes
Cooking Time: 4 hours 20 minutes
Servings: 5
Ingredients:

- 5 pounds trimmed turkey
- 5 tablespoons Ras el Hanout (Moroccan Spice Blend) seasoning
- Kosher salt
- Zest of 3 lemons
- 1 cup olive oil
- Mint leaves

Directions:

1. Cut the backbone of turkey and remove the spine and discard the fat.
2. Flip the turkey breast-side up and press into the breastbone to flatten it
3. Then rub the turkey with oil and then massage the seasoning along with salt and lemon zest.
4. Seal the turkey with plastic wrap and marinate it for 30 minutes.
5. Heat the smoker for 20 minutes.
6. Soak the wood chip in water one hour before smoking.
7. Remove plastic wrap and cook the turkey for 4 hours 20 minutes at 250 degrees F.
8. Garnish it with mint leaves.

Nutrition:
Calories 1062
Total Fat 72.7g
Saturated Fat 15.9g
Cholesterol 284mg
Sodium 1660mg
Total Carbohydrate 3.8g
Dietary Fiber 2.2g
Total Sugars 1.5g
Protein 85.2g
Calcium 45mg
Iron 1mg
Potassium 10mg

210. Turkey with Chimichurri

Preparation Time: 1 hour 10 minutes
Cooking Time: 4 hours
Servings: 5
Ingredients:

- 5 pounds bone-in, skin on turkey pieces
- Salt and pepper
- 1teaspoon paprika
- ½ teaspoon cayenne
- 2 tablespoons olive oil
- 1 pepper
- 1 onion
- 2 carrots, chopped
- 2 scallions
- 2 tomatoes, chopped
- Homemade Chimichurri Sauce
- ½ cup olive oil
- 1 teaspoon parsley
- 1 teaspoon red pepper flakes
- 2 garlic cloves
- 2 red onions

Directions:

1. Season the washed and clean turkey with the salt, pepper, paprika and cayenne pepper.
2. Rub it gently all over.
3. Arrange the wood chip inside the smoker and then Heat the smoker to 230 degrees F.
4. Transfer the turkey to the sheet pan and arrange peppers, onions, carrots, scallion, and tomatoes beside it.
5. Drizzle the olive oil on top.
6. Place the pan sheet inside the smoker.
7. Close the electric smoker door and then cook for 4 hours at 250 degrees F.
8. Check the turkey to an internal temperature of 165F.
9. Now, it is time to make the chimichurri.
10. Blend all the homemade chimichurri ingredients in a blender and puree until combined.
11. Serve the cooked turkey and veggie with the ready to serve the sauce.

Nutrition:
Calories 807
Total Fat 35.9g
Saturated Fat 4.5g
Cholesterol 283mg
Sodium 920mg
Total Carbohydrate 11.7g
Dietary Fiber 2.9g
Total Sugars 5.8g
Protein 94.8g
Calcium 32mg
Iron 6mg
Potassium 311mg

211. Whole Smoked Turkey Recipe
Preparation Time: 16 hours
Cooking Time: 10 hours
Servings: 14
Ingredients:

- ½ cup salt
- 1/3 cup molasses
- 1/3 cup granulated sugar
- ½ cup Worcestershire sauce
- 6 cloves, smashed garlic
- 4 dried bay leaves
- Black pepper to taste
- 14 pounds whole turkey
- 2 cups bourbon
- 1 cup canola oil for coating

Directions:

1. Pour a gallon of water, salt, sugar, molasses, garlic, Worcestershire sauce, bourbon, pepper, and bay leaves in a large pot.
2. Boil for a few minutes and then cool it down completely.
3. Submerge the turkey completely in the brine using a large bucket.
4. Brine it in the liquid for 15 hours.
5. The next day, take the turkey out of the brine and pat dry with paper towel.
6. Rub the turkey with oil and additional pepper.
7. Load the smoker with soaked wood chips, and place the turkey inside the smoker for cooking.
8. Set temperature to 250 degrees F.
9. Once the internal temperate is 165 degrees F, the turkey is ready.
10. Note: It took about 10 hours of cooking.

Nutrition:
Calories 770 Total Fat 29.2g
Saturated Fat 1.7g
Cholesterol 249mg
Sodium 9583mg
Total Carbohydrate 47.8g
Dietary Fiber 1.9g
Total Sugars 29g
Protein 61.3g
Calcium 95mg
Iron 10mg
Potassium 1705mg

212. Classic Smoked Turkey Recipe
Preparation Time: 30 minutes
Cooking Time: 12 hours
Servings: 16
Ingredients:

- 16 pounds turkey

- 2 tablespoons dried thyme
- 1 tablespoon dried sage
- 2 teaspoons dried oregano
- 2 teaspoons paprika
- 1 tablespoon sea salt
- Black pepper, to taste
- 1 teaspoon dried rosemary
- Zest of 1 orange
- 1/3 cup extra-virgin olive oil
- 1/3 cup apple cider
- 1/3 cups water

Directions:
1. Heat the electric smoker to 250 degrees F.
2. Take a small bowl and mix all the dry spices and ingredients.
3. Rub it gently over the turkey meat.
4. At the end drizzle olive oil on top.
5. Now pour water along with apple cider in the large water pan in the bottom of the electric smoker.
6. Place a drip pan on the next rack or shelf of the smoker.
7. Fill the sides with the apple wood chips.
8. Move the turkey on the top rack of the smoker.
9. Close the rack and then cook for approximately 12 hours.
10. Add more wood if smoke stops coming.
11. Use the digital probe thermometer to get an internal temperature of 165 degrees F.
12. Remove the turkey and serve.

Nutrition:
Total Fat 27g
Saturated Fat 8.1g
Cholesterol 343mg
Sodium 669mg
Total Carbohydrate 2.6g
Dietary Fiber 0.7g
Total Sugars 1.7g
Calories 818
Protein 133.1g
Calcium 31mg
Iron 46mg
Potassium 1393mg

213. Turkey in the Electric Smoker

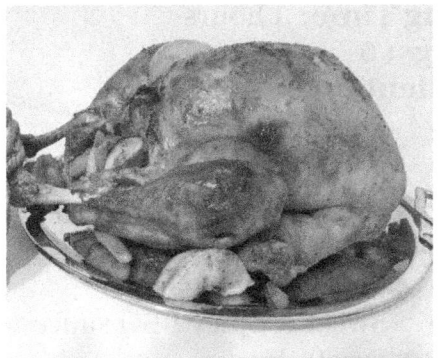

Preparation Time: 1 hour 10 minutes
Cooking Time: 10 hours
Servings: 10
Ingredients:
- 1 (10 pounds) whole turkey
- 4 cloves garlic, crushed
- 2 tablespoons salt, seasoned
- ½ cup butter
- 1 (12 fluid ounce) cola-flavored carbonated beverage
- 1 apple, quartered
- 1 onion, quartered
- 1 tablespoon garlic powder
- 1 tablespoon salt
- 1 tablespoon black pepper

Directions:
1. Heat the electric smoker to 225F and then rinse the turkey well under water, pat dry and then rub it with seasoned salt.
2. Place it inside a roasting pan.
3. Combine cola, butter, apples, garlic powder, salt, and pepper in a bowl .
4. Fill the cavity of turkey with cola, apples, garlic powder, salt, and pepper. Rub butter and crushed garlic outside of the turkey as well.
5. Cover the turkey with foil. Smoke the turkey for 10 hours at 250 degrees F. Once it's done, serve.

Nutrition:
Calories 907 Total Fat 63.2g
Saturated Fat 22.3g Cholesterol 4256mg
Sodium 2364mg Total Carbohydrate 17.9g
Dietary Fiber 1.1g Total Sugars 9.7g
Protein 62.7g Calcium 462mg
Iron 19mg Potassium 710mg

214. Smoked Turkey Legs
Preparation Time: 15 minutes
Cooking Time: 4 hours
Servings: 6
Ingredients:

- 6 turkey legs
- 3 tsp. Worcestershire sauce
- 1 tbsp. vegetable oil
- Dry Rub, recipe follows
- Mop, recipe follows
- Sweet & Spicy BBQ sauce
- Dry Rub:
- 1/4 cup chipotle seasoning, (recommended: North of the Border Chipotle Seasoning)
- 1 to 2 tsp. mild dried ground red chili or paprika
- 1 tbsp. packed brown sugar
- Mop Mixture:
- 1 cup white vinegar
- 1 tbsp. BBQ Sauce, (recommended: North of the Border Chipotle Barbecue Sauce)

Directions:

1. Loosen the skin of the turkey legs beforehand. You can do this by running your fingers under it
2. Mix together the oil and Worcestershire sauce. Rub the mixture over the turkey legs. Be sure to get some of it under the skin. Next, sprinkle the rub over the legs.
3. Put the legs in a plastic bag. Store in the fridge.
4. Take out the turkey legs from the fridge. Allow them to sit out for half an hour so they come up to room temperature.
5. Warm up the mop mixture.
6. Place the turkey legs in the smoker. Be sure to mop the legs every 45 minutes.
7. Once the turkey legs are done, serve them hot. They're best eaten with your fingers with some barbeque sauce. Smoke Temp: 220

Nutrition:
Calories 203
Total Fat 9.6g
Saturated Fat 2.7g
Cholesterol 63mg
Sodium 233mg
Total Carbohydrate 5.4g
Dietary Fiber 0.2g
Total Sugars 4.7g
Protein 20.6g
Vitamin D 0mcg
Calcium 29mg
Iron 2mg
Potassium 244mg

215. Brined Whole Turkey
Preparation Time: 24 hours
Cooking Time: 12 hours
Servings: 15
Ingredients:

- 2 cups kosher salt
- 6 cups water, 1/4 cup black pepper corns
- 3 tablespoons chopped garlic cloves
- 2 tablespoons chopped basil leaves
- 2 tablespoons onion powder
- 1/2 cup soy sauce, 1/2 cup Worcestershire sauce
- 1/4 cup extra virgin olive oil
- 10 pounds whole turkey

Directions:

1. In a large stockpot, mix together salt, water, pepper corn, garlic, and basil. Heat until the salt dissolves. Let it cool.
2. Submerge the turkey into the brine solution and put in the fridge for 24 hours.
3. Pour out the brine and rinse the water completely. Pat dry.
4. In a bowl, combine the onion powder, soy sauce, Worcestershire sauce, and olive oil.
5. Brush onto the entire surface of the turkey.
6. Heat the smoker to 225F.

7. Place water in the water pan then add maple wood chips into the side tray. Place turkey in the smoker. Cook for 12 hours.

Nutrition:
Calories 525
Total Fat 25g
Saturated Fat 7.2g
Cholesterol 189mg
Sodium 16543mg
Total Carbohydrate 2g
Dietary Fiber 0.2g
Total Sugars 0.5
Protein 57.4g
Vitamin D 0mcg
Calcium 21mg
Iron 0mg
Potassium 39mg

216. Honey Smoked Turkey
Preparation Time: 6 minutes
Cooking Time: 6 hours
Servings: 7
Ingredients:
- 1 gallon of hot water
- 1 pound of kosher salt
- 2 quarts of vegetable broth
- 8 ounce jars of honey
- 1 cup of orange juice
- 7 pound bag of ice cubes
- 15 pound of whole turkey with giblets and neck removed
- ¼ cup of vegetable oil
- 1 teaspoon of poultry seasoning
- 1 granny smith apples cored and cut up into large chunks
- 1 celery stalk cut up into small chunks
- 1 small sized onion cut up into chunks
- 1 quartered orange

Directions:
1. Take a 54 quart cooler and add kosher salt and hot water
2. Mix them well until everything dissolves
3. Add vegetable broth, orange juice and honey
4. Pour ice cubes into the mix and add the turkey into your brine, keeping the breast side up
5. Lock up the lid of your cooler and let it marinate overnight for 12 hours
6. Make sure that the brine temperature stays under 40 degree Fahrenheit
7. Remove the turkey from the brine then discard the brine
8. Dry the turkey using a kitchen towel
9. Take a bowl then mix vegetable oil and poultry seasoning
10. Rub the turkey with the mixture
11. Place apple, onion, celery and orange pieces inside the cavity of the turkey
12. Pre-heat your smoker to a temperature of 400 degree Fahrenheit and add 1 cup of hickory wood chips
13. Set your turkey onto your smoker and insert a probe into the thickest part of your turkey breast
14. Set the probe for 160 degree Fahrenheit
15. Smoke the turkey for 2 hours until the skin is golden brown
16. Cover the breast, wings and legs using aluminum foil and keep smoking it for 2-3 hours until the probe thermometer reads 160 degree Fahrenheit
17. Make sure to keep adding some hickory chips to your heat box occasionally
18. Remove the vegetables and fruit from the cavity of your Turkey and cover it up with aluminum foil
19. Let it rest of 1 hour and carve it up!

Nutrition:
Calories: 353
Fats: 16g
Carbs: 29g
Fiber: 2g

217. Turkey Salad

Preparation Time: 24 hours 20 minutes
Cooking Time: 5 hours
Servings: 8
Ingredients:

- 1 (4 lbs.)turkey breast
- 6 tbsp. extra-virgin olive oil
- 3 tbsp. fresh thyme, chopped
- 3 tbsp. white wine vinegar
- 2 qts. apple juice
- 2 qts. water
- 2 tbsp. lemon juice
- 2 ½ cups dried cherries, chopped
- 1 cup kosher salt
- 1 cup brown sugar
- 1 cup green onions, chopped
- ½ cup maple syrup
- ¾ cup celery, chopped
- ½ cup mayonnaise
- 8-oz. package mixed baby greens
- ½ cup toasted hazelnuts, coarsely chopped
- Salt and black pepper, to taste

Directions:

1. To prepare the brine, mix the salt, brown sugar, syrup, apple juice and water in a stockpot. Put the turkey breast in the prepared mixture and refrigerate for 12-24 hours.
2. Heat the electric smoker to 225F. Put one small handful of prepared wood chips in the wood tray.
3. Clean the meat of remaining brine mixture. Rinse well.
4. Put the turkey breast on the middle rack of the smoker. Cook for 25 to 30 mins until the internal temperature reaches 165° F.
5. Let it cool for 15 mins.

6. To prepare the salad, combine sliced or chopped turkey breast, green onions, celery, mayonnaise, 2 tbsp. thyme, and lemon juice and stir well.
7. For the vinaigrette, blend oil, vinegar, and the remaining thyme in a salad bowl. Add salt and pepper to taste.
8. Toss the greens in this mixture. Serve the turkey salad on top of the greens and top with cherries and nuts.

Nutrition:
Calcium, Ca142 mg
Magnesium, Mg114 mg
Phosphorus, P586 mg
Iron, Fe5.83 mg
Potassium, K1162 mg
Sodium, Na14575 mg
Zinc, Zn5.28 mg

218. Smoked Turkey & Sausage Gumbo

Preparation Time: 25 hours
Cooking Time: 8 hours
Servings: 12
Ingredients:

- 1 (10-12 lb.) smoked turkey, bought
- 8 cups water
- 3 cloves garlic, minced
- 2 tbsp. green onions, chopped
- 2 tbsp. fresh parsley leaves, chopped
- 2 cups coarsely chopped yellow onions
- 2 celery stalks
- 1 tsp. fresh thyme, chopped
- 1 cup celery, coarsely chopped
- 1 cup green bell peppers, chopped
- 1½ lbs. andouille or smoked sausage, sliced
- 1½ cups canola oil
- 1½ cups bleached all-purpose flour
- Poultry rub
- Hot cooked white rice (for serving)
- Salt, pepper

Directions:

1. Brine the turkey for no longer than 24 hours, using your favorite brine, bought or homemade. Spice Hunter Turkey Brine is advisable. Clean the poultry from remaining brine mixture. Rinse well inside and out.
2. Heat the electric smoker to 250F. Put one small handful of prepared wood chips in the wood tray; for the best result use a combination of hickory and apple.
3. Smoke the turkey until the temperature inside the turkey meat reaches 180F.
4. Remove the turkey and cut the meat from the bones. Reserve the meat aside.
5. Mix water, celery stalks, onion, garlic cloves in a large stockpot.
6. Put the turkey carcass in this mixture and boil for 1 hr. Strain the broth.
7. Combine oil and flour in another pot. Cook the mixture on low for about 25 mins. , stirring often until a dark roux is formed. Add the onions, bell peppers, celery, and garlic. Mix the ingredients well and cook for another 10 mins. Add the thyme and cayenne.
8. Add the smoked turkey broth and combine well, stirring constantly. Cook on medium heat for 1½ hrs. Add water, if needed.
9. Chop the smoked turkey meat. Add the turkey and the sausage to the gumbo. Cook for another 30 mins. Season with salt and pepper to taste.
10. Set aside, then skim off the fat from the surface.
11. Serve over hot white rice in gumbo or soup bowls.

Nutrition:
Calcium, Ca78 mg Magnesium, Mg38 mg
Phosphorus, P201 mg
Iron, Fe3.65 mg Potassium, K290 mg
Sodium, Na532 mg Zinc, Zn1.7 mg

219. Sweet Smokey Turkey with Herbs

Preparation Time: 30 minutes
Cooking Time: 1 hour 20 minutes
Servings: 10
Ingredients:

* 1 Whole Turkey
* 2½ tbsps. Sage
* 1½ tbsps. Black pepper
* 1½ tsps. Salt
* 2½ tbsps. Basil
* 2½ tbsps. Olive oil
* ¾ c. raw honey

Directions:

1. Heat the electric smoker to 225°F (107°C). Don't forget to soak the wood chips in water before using them.
2. Carefully wash and clean the turkey then place in the roasting pan.
3. Combine sage with black pepper, salt, basil, and olive oil then mix until incorporated.
4. Rub the turkey with the spice mixture then wrap it with aluminum foil.
5. Place the wrapped turkey on the electric smoker rack then close the smoker's lid.
6. Cook the turkey for 50 minutes then take it out from the smoker.
7. Unwrap the turkey then brush all sides of the turkey with raw honey.
8. Re-wrap the glazed turkey with aluminum foil then return back to the electric smoker.
9. Add about 2 handfuls of soaked mesquites wood chips and cook the turkey for 2 hours more or until the internal temperature has reached 180°F (80°C).
10. Once the turkey is done, remove from the electric smoker then unwrap it.
11. Brush the turkey with the remaining honey then cook again without cover for about 20 minutes. This process is done to darken the turkey.

12. Once it is done, take the turkey out from the electric smoker then place on a serving dish.
13. Serve and enjoy.

Nutrition:
Calories: 312
Total fat: 9g
Net carbs: 1g
Protein: 55g

220. Apple Cola Smoked Turkey
Preparation Time: 15 minutes
Cooking Time: 9 hours
Servings: 10
Ingredients:

- 5 lbs. Whole Turkey
- 3 tbsps. Minced garlic
- 2½ tbsps. Salt
- ¾ c. Butter
- 3 cans carbonated beverage with cola flavor
- 2 Fresh apples
- ½ c. Chopped onion
- 3 tsps. Garlic powder
- 1½ tsps. Black pepper

Directions:

1. Heat the electric smoker to 225°F (110°C).
2. Meanwhile, rub the turkey with rub ingredients then place in a disposable pan. Set aside.
3. Cut the apple into cubes then place in a bowl.
4. Add chopped onion, garlic powder, butter, and black pepper to the bowl then pour the carbonated beverage. Mix well.
5. Fill the turkey with the apple mixture then cover with aluminum foil.
6. Place the pan in the smoker then smoke the turkey for 9 hours.
7. Brush the turkey with juice from the filling every 2 hours.
8. After 9 hours or when the internal temperature has reached 180°F (80°C), remove the smoked turkey from the smoker.
9. Cool for a few minutes then serve.
10. Cut into slices then enjoy.

Nutrition:
Calories: 625
Total fat: 31.7g
Net carbs: 9.8g
Protein: 71.2g

221. Savory Herb Rubbed and Aromatic Stuffed Smoked Turkey Recipe
Preparation Time: 15 minutes
Cooking Time: 7 hours
Servings: 16
Ingredients:

- 3 TBS extra virgin olive oil (EVOO)
- 3 TBS unsalted butter at room temperature
- 1/2 cup apple cider (might need more)
- 1 lemon or orange cut in quarters
- 2 cloves fresh garlic minced
- 2 TBS dried thyme
- 12 to 14 pound turkey
- 1 TBS powdered sage
- 2 tsps dried oregano
- 2 tsps paprika
- 1-1/2 tsps cracked black pepper
- 1 tsp dried rosemary
- 1 apple cut in quarters
- 1 medium onion cut in half
- 1/2 cup water
- 2 tsps sea salt

Directions:

1. Line a drip pan and water bowl with aluminum foil for easier cleanup. Heat the smoker to 225F.
2. In a small bowl, cream together the EVOO and softened butter. Mix in the garlic, herbs, and spices.
3. Rub the interior cavity of the turkey with 1/3 of this mixture. Stuff the cavity with the fruits and onion. Rub the outside of the bird with the remaining fat and herb blend.
4. Place the water and apple cider to fill the water pan half way. Place the drip pan on the next rack just above the water pan to collect drippings from the turkey. Fill the side tray with the wood chips.

5. Tuck the tips of the wings tightly beneath the turkey. Place the seasoned turkey directly on the middle rack of the smoker. Insert the digital thermometer into the thigh of the bird, if your smoker has one. Set a timer for approximately 6.5 hours. A turkey generally smokes for 30 to 40 minutes per pound. You want to achieve an inside temperature of 165F.

6. Check the vent every hour for smoke. Add more wood chips if the smoke has died down. Also, check the water pan and add addition cider and water as needed.

7. Start checking the internal temperature of the bird after 3 or 4 hours and every 45 minutes thereafter with either the digital thermometer or a good meat thermometer.

8. Remove the cooked turkey to a cutting board and allow it to rest for a minimum of 20 minutes before carving. You can tent it with aluminum foil to keep more moisture in.

Nutrition:
Calories 618
Total Fat 19.8g
Saturated Fat 6g
Cholesterol 258mg
Sodium 473mg
Total Carbohydrate 4.3g
Dietary Fiber 0.9g
Total Sugars 2.6g
Protein 99.9g
Vitamin D 0mcg
Calcium 24mg
Iron 35mg
Potassium 1065mg

Conclusion

Did you enjoy smoking your favorite meat, fish, vegetables, and others you thought of to cook in your Electric Smoker? Then, thank you for choosing this fantastic cookbook! Indeed, you have learned a lot from knowing your Electric Smoker better, to its maintenance, and trying some of the recipes in this cookbook. If you educate yourself on Electric Smokers' features, you will have an easy time sorting through all of the choices available and find the one that will fit your cooking needs the best. Electric Smokers provide another way to cook meat and other food uniquely and deliciously.

With this cookbook, all you have to do is take action and proceed with your Electric Smoker's barbequing journey. So start cooking! The only thing that you need is the ingredients showed in this Electric Smoker cookbook. Grab your Electric Smoker, this cookbook, and you will enjoy the process of smoking food in your Electric Smoker! Cheers, and welcome to the world of electric smoking!

- You can cook more food with an Electric Smoker than using a gas grill or even charcoal, but this will only cost you less on electricity.
- You start cooking faster because this cooking process takes less time!
- You can be sure that the food you are preparing is cooked evenly and thoroughly; hence, healthily!
- You can have delicious smoked food without smelling bad-burn inside your house!
- Your outdoor Electric Smoker is very safe because it does not produce dangerous gases. You can start cooking with your family, and your children can be watching while cooking!
- Your outdoor Electric Smoker does not overheat, and it is durable, which means that you can save your hard-earned cash from other buying worries!
- There is a lot of recipes in this cookbook, and you will be able to cook different kinds of grill-smoked dishes!
- You don't have to fret about your Electric Smoker, and its design is ingenious since it operates cleanly!

There you go! Now you are confident in cooking in your Electric Smoker, thank this cookbook guide and the benefits you have experienced from your purchase! Remember, you have enjoyed cooking with organic ingredients, and the most important thing is that you can be assured of your own health.

Even if you have never used an Electric Smoker before, it is not difficult to learn how to use it, and the delicious meals you cook in it will impress your family and friends. If you are new to this kind of unique appliance, this cookbook will enlighten you through your Electric Smoking journey! As for this last guide, we will talk about the benefits you have gained with your Electric Smoker and this cookbook:

Finally, you are trusted by families to cook for them, and so many people who know about your Electric Smoker can enjoy what you have prepared for them. It is better to go back to the cookbook to learn more about your Electric Smoker and all the nutritious dishes that you can cook in it from time to time. Share this cookbook with your family, friends, and co-workers, and be sure that you have the best entertaining way to cook in your Electric Smoker!

Made in the USA
Las Vegas, NV
09 June 2024

90927109R00077